SANTIAGO NETRI

WHAT DOES MONEY MEAN IN YOUR LIFE?

Dare to design your future

SANTIAGO NETRI

Netri, Santiago
What does money mean in your life? Dare to design your future
Santiago Netri. - 1st ed. - Santiago Netri,
280 p.; 23 x 15 cm.

ISBN 979-832-61904-0-6
Amazon Spanish ISBN Paperback: 979-885-33974-8-4
Amazon Spanish ISBN Hardcover: 979-885-33931-7-2

1. Microeconomics. 2. Personal Finances. I. Title.
CDD 332.024

Published by SNM Publishers
Amazon Kindle Direct Publishing

v. 43.798

All rights reserved. Total or partial reproduction of this work by any means or procedure is prohibited without the written permission of the author.
No part of this book may be reproduced or compiled on a computer system without the prior written permission of the copyright owner.
Book printed on demand (print on demand) at the author's request.

First edition in English: SNM Publishers 2024
First edition in Spanish: SNM Publishers 2023

The first people I dedicate this book to are my parents, who at some point decided to give me the opportunity to live, and begin to walk this path of abundance, which today I am beginning to identify more clearly.

To all the experiences that allowed me to get frustrated and made me realize that I needed to make changes in my life.

To all the people, loved ones and professionals, who marked directions and opportunities for me to design.

To my wife and family, who accompany me in the process of manifesting these contents, providing good observations and the necessary encouragement to always move forward.

SANTIAGO NETRI

Thank you for purchasing this book.

Are your goals big enough?

If we are going to climb the stair, we have to make sure that the steps are in good condition, allowing us to climb.

If I want to go to the upper level but I can't find the stairs; in that case, where is the elevator?

We use the steps to climb, they are the path to true learning.

Questions about ABUNDANCE

I understand that it is logical that you consider that Money is part of Abundance, it may not be so, answer the following questions:

What comes to your mind when I name the word abundance?

_____

_____

Today, what aspect of your life is abundant?

_____

_____

Think about what your abundant life would be like. Imagine it, enjoy it, write down what comes to you.

_____

_____

Why are you starting to read this book? Is it associated with the concept of abundance?

_____

_____

Index

Introduction 13
    1st part: **Revise** 18
    2nd part: **Action** 19
    3rd part: **Learn** 19
    4th part: **Practice and develop habits** 20
PART 1 21
Review! 21
  Motivation to change 23
  How you perceive Money 27
  Know your beliefs (danger) 37
  Finding the dinosaur doesn't change you 41
  The commands condition you. Have you already discovered them? 46
  Lack and Abundance 49
  Let's review the doing 57
  Synthesis 1 60
PART 2 63
Take action! 63
  Have a coffee with money 65
  Dare to change 73
  Bridges to change 82

    Your dreams suffer from inflation 86
    Interest is the measure of action 89
    Design your new habits 95
    What is important is uncomfortable 101
    Emotional management 107
    Educate your mind and your heart 113
    Synthesis 2 121
PART 3 123
Learn! 123
    Financial education 125
    The four ways of living 132
    The four keys of a rich man 142
    Your profit is always your surplus 174
    If time is not enough, you are in lack 184
    Managing abundance 190
    The debt of the one who looses and the one who wins 199
    You write the future 205
    Synthesis 3 208
PART 4 211
Practice! Develop habits! 211
    Methodology to change 213

Warnings 301
Nobody is a prophet in their own land 305
Cross the surf 309
Your talent is valued in the right context 313
Balance is what defines your freedom 317
Synthesis 4 321
Integration 325
Epilogue 329
Attachments 331
Courage and Fear 333
Time 340
Santiago Netri 345

Introduction

Value Question

A few years ago, I honestly asked myself the following question, *what does money mean in my life?*

From there began a path that, close to being associated with money in factual terms, turned out to be quite a work of **psycho-emotional, and perceptual** revision of how money had traveled and impacted my life story.

The first thing I was able to review is that money as a general concept, immersed and part of civilizations, is in itself an "archetype" of the collective unconscious.

That means, it is something that we all interpret and know what it is and what it is for, with specific characteristics and functions.

Now, my first important discovery was to understand more deeply that, while we all understand what money is archetypically, **we give it an individual and unique meaning for us.**

The title and question that lead this book are individual for each person and it is one who finds its own meaning.

How does the journey of money begin?

Money has an individual history in how it has traveled in different countries; the perceptual concept given to it in Argentina or in other latitudes is not the same; the money is the same, but it is perceived in different ways. It is important to understand that when we are born in a particular country, we are influenced by the culture of the place we belong.

Money as a collective and cultural archetype also begins to move closer to us, in the family in which we are born, where it circulates with particularities; perhaps in some cases with abundance, in others with scarcity, with negligence, with planning, in short..., with very unique codes and beliefs of each "group," from which one absorbs its conception almost by osmosis.

So: it is a universal archetype, which has specific meanings associated with the culture of a country and the family ecosystem that each person inhabits; however:

How do we get to our own interpretation of it?

We internalize the concepts of life when we begin to have our own real experiences.

How these experiences are experienced, with what emotions, with what results (good or bad), with what interactions and vitality, our perceptual and cognitive system remembers (introjects) a meaning, a value to those experiences and the concepts that make them up.

For example: if in a person's life history, assets were lost in the family home when they were going through adolescence, this experience has an impact, a relevant psycho-emotional influence, and a specific significance associated with the lived experience; therefore, money, which is **"the means by which one acquires goods,"** is decidedly affected in its significance.

In the seminars that I hold, we not only review what it means today, a priori for each person, but we also promote a work of redefinition of the particular experiences that conditioned that representation in each case, in order to **give "money" its true meaning**, *an exchange good to acquire what I need and want.*

This allows us to elaborate not only the conditioning emotional knot, but also the limiting and enabling beliefs, both about a particular event and/or also those carried by each family tree in its ancestry.

Therefore, **we always have a meaning of money**. The good thing about having it is that we can review it and see if it is consistent with what we want and long for in life at the moment. The interesting thing about a meaning, whatever it may be, is that we can redefine it; as a result of learning, we manage to assimilate new ways of perceiving something in life, and this is what decisively makes us creators and evolutionary beings.

I have accompanied and experienced amazing transformations in this sense.

Once an effective redefinition (psycho-emotional and perceptual) of some concept is carried out, we quickly try to project it into life by changing our surrounding reality, but this work is not only perceptual, it is very important that after redefining, to learn new knowledge to structure the new present and build our future; not entering into a learning path can be risky, one tends to easily fall into "magical thinking," which always leads to many frustrations.

We are always projecting our internal meanings into reality, we construct realities, so to speak, according to our framework of meaning.

That is why I emphasize that our first step should be reviewing if the meaning money has for us today is coherent and congruent with what we long for; if not, I suggest you venture to the question that leads these paragraphs:

What meaning does money have in your life?

How is this book organized?

I will share with you what I have been doing on this topic, I want to tell you about the 4 main parts that will serve as a common thread to assist, associate, and accompany the reading and understanding of the created purpose.

1st part: **Revise**

The first block of chapters guides the topic and focuses on beginning to understand what money means in our lives and how this happens objectively. I consider these chapters of great importance, since without this conscious record, it is very difficult to make lasting changes on this topic and any other. Although the focus is $$, the information provided will serve to detect and elaborate other aspects as well.

Understanding how we perceive, how we signify, how we make our limiting and enabling beliefs, how the emotional dimension affects our reality and how we begin to design the new habits that are what allow real change.

I have read many books associated with the topic of money, and really there are very few that delve into how to take the knowledge they explain and implement it in a concrete and practical way, allowing sustainable changes. That is why we will dedicate time at the beginning of this book to understand and experience from where we perceive, interpret and change our lives.

2nd part: **Action**

We will focus on our actions and how we create change. Here we will break paradigms. For example: "Does introspection into causes solve things?" Honoring the great power of the human being, we will show some possibilities of how to generate the new. Excessive introspection limits action, the opposite does too, a balance is necessary, prioritizing ACTION. The resolution of a challenge is not resolved only with theories and thoughts, it is resolved when our being takes action.

How an intention to change can be part of a new behavior, a new habit, a new way of living. Money will be an important character in this film; the main actors are us.

3rd part: **Learn**

I will present specific knowledge on the topic. We will incorporate "ways of looking" at the different phases of the money flow, we will channel the review of financial concepts, which are not always used clearly;

I will comment on specific experiences and cases to exemplify what is stated. We will navigate in learning from logic, applying knowledge in a practical way and incorporating displacements into our learning.

These "ways of looking" will give us perspective and objectivity, even within the daily subjectivity of our work.

4th part: **Practice and develop habits**

The importance of being methodical and going deeper into our actions to achieve what we are looking for. Order and time management are critical factors when we want to develop a habit. You have to follow a method, be consistent and constant.

I will present some maxims (research topics) so that they can be correctly applied. At the end, an integrative chapter will be presented, that will allow us to address the journey taken in a 360-degree (integral) manner.

PART 1

Review!

SANTIAGO NETRI

Motivation to change

$

Starting

In my early years, and even after my youth, I believed that I was not interested in money. I observed a lot of stress in people who had it, but at the same time enjoyed realities that gave sensations of freedom and ease. Contradictions appeared in my mind. I felt those lives of "freedom" were foreign, far from my possibilities, I stayed inside my comfort zone, I thought to myself *"money is not an interest for me"* and told myself the old tale of *"what matters is our interior."* **Everything is important, what is inside and what is outside, because it is our life.** Today, writing these paragraphs, I realize that the issue of money affected me, generating impacts of pain and vulnerability, which still mobilize me to this day. **To say that money is of little importance, I would consider foolishness today.**

Perhaps it was for this reason, now that I reflect on it, that I was dedicated from an early age in educating myself in different arts, where I recreated for many years a creative dimension, which today I still preserve and value as central and transcendent, but where money was not the main character.

I then began to have different experiences related to this concept ($) in my family, and I was able to experience dysfunction and confusion in certain circumstances that occurred, both in economic and emotional terms. I understood that money could not be left out, that its presence gave peace of mind or despair to different people around me.

My internal concerns led me vocationally to my role as a psychological consultant, where I observed the implication that economic life has on the different consultants I receive; detecting the lack of clarity we have in this regard, and the consequences generated by not handling this issue in depth. Currently, in my activity as an organizational consultant, I confirm this premise even more.

Finally, I determinedly set out to investigate my relationship with this topic in my own life story, addressing my initial contradictions. I definitely came to the importance and relevance of money, and how it is closely related to our balance in life, with our moments of joy and sadness, how it goes through all activities, personal and work; the past, present and future intermingle in knots that require money on the other side of the scale.

My motivation, then, starts from sharing a multiplicity of aspects that I discovered and deepened, which is a product of what I initially **experienced** and **observed** in my environment, of what **I learn by accompanying** consultants and clients, which **I discover by going deeper** in my life and what I still **assimilate** when I try to **provide, explain and train** others.

I read in a book by Robin Sharma, that an entrepreneur had lied saying that she had gone to a seminar to learn, I stopped reading, then continued, and I read that the real reason as to why she was there was that she needed to regain hope and save her life. Yes, this is what it is about, it is the meaning we give to our experiences and our desires that will determine how that hope will grow until it becomes a habit of healthy roots and actions.

What I long for is that whoever can understand and connect with some concepts and experiences that are in this book, will be able to create their own meaning, and from there, can give more comprehensive and concrete importance to the "real value" that this archetype ($) contains, of so much importance in our daily lives.

Start by avoiding phrases that indicate that you are not interested in something, and even

more so if that is something that you live with every day.
Words sustain the strength of inner energy, and when we use them in a negative way, we defocus on what really interests us.
Let's express what does interest us.
If we are athletes, does it make sense to say that we are not interested in nutrition? Food is related to sports performance, as money is to our daily lives.

How you perceive Money

$

Psychology of Money

As we clarified in the introduction of this book, we are people who give meaning to life based on the experiences we go through; these, by impacting our cognitive-perceptual system, generate particular "signs," giving it a unique content meaning for each one of us.

Next, we will explain in a simple and practical way how we come to mean:

Every idea (for example "the idea of a car") is an archetype of the collective unconscious, that is, something that we all identify, knowing its functions and characteristics; the same thing happens with "the idea of money," or with the signs ($) that represent it.

This idea, which is already an archetype, is colored by the cultural environment where it circulates (country of residence). As we clarified in the introduction, the meaning of money in Argentina is not the same as in other countries. This aspect also helps our cognitive-perceptual system begin to receive information with particular nuances.

From our approach, the greatest point of implication is when the concept of money enters the orbit of our family of origin; since there it's not only experienced in a particular way, but everything experienced in our family network has a strong emotional component for us. Which means that the experiences we go through at this point have a relevant impact on our perceptual system.

It is for this reason that we associate the significance with *"the psychology of money,"* giving it an important framework to be able to review our life history, and deepen how the different experiences that we go through as children, during adolescence, in youth and adulthood, and even those that our ancestors have experienced in the family branch, impact and carry information, which is symbolized by our perceptual system.

Depending on how certain experiences have been experienced, they leave meaning in our psyche.

For example: If a family finds it difficult to "make ends meet," that is, to be able to cover basic fixed costs; it is very likely that the meaning of money has perceptions of scarcity, sacrifice, excessive effort, "it is never enough" mindset, etc. Here it is important to note that there is no gratitude for what we have, but rather the scarcity of getting to the "end of the month" the predominant factor in this thinking.

Or on the contrary, a very wealthy family, where it is known that the origin of the money is not entirely legal; surely the meaning framework makes some members think that money is "dirty," "that those who have $ cheat," etc.

Lack of perspective: with the budget that a family that "barely" makes it has, others can live comfortably, or others not even for a few moments. Meaning has implicit perspective. There are positive meanings that can be presented, where the concept of **money and the real possibilities it offers,** favors us.

In the training workshops that I carry out, I usually ask what the words they associate the concept of money with are; and how each person means differently; the answers are very varied:

Let's reflect that behind each meaningful word there are stories that determine it and there is a perceptual system symbolizing it.

Once we find the **meaning**, we create with that concept ($) an **internal relationship**, almost as if we had a friend, with whom we relate, interact and have concrete dialogues. That is why in one of the chapters of this book I metaphorically invite the reader to "have coffee with money," and ask: who is it?

If I have lack meanings with respect to $, I will always "dialogue" to myself that things are expensive, that I will never earn more than what I need; worse still, it will distance me from gratitude, towards oneself and towards others.

That internal relationship generated will then pass to an instance of **projection**.

The latter is a process by which the perception of the human being has the property of creating, of projecting outside what is perceived inside, what has meaning (like an image projector). Therefore, if I mean abundance in relation to money, I will project into my environment realities where abundance is present.

The phrase "that each person creates their reality" is totally true and logical. We create our reality from our meanings (in future chapters we will develop this).

Process:

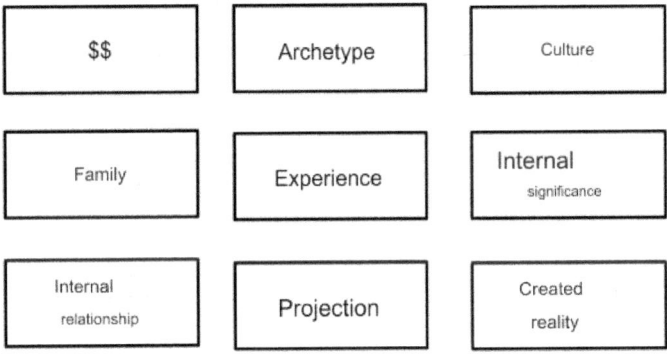

Just as it happens with money, it happens with other concepts that we are experimenting with. The first step is to realize that everything we have conceptualized is somehow meant; and the meanings can be accepted, modified, renewed and updated, but never denied. "Acceptance of our reality is the beginning of change."

Exercise

Next, I invite you to perform an exercise that will be of great importance to identify experiences in our life history that are related to the history of money.

I propose to make a chronological timeline from when you were born to the present, where you can detect and list relevant experiences (both positive and negative) that you can, and feel are connected to money.

Examples:

    a. My parents sent me to a new school because they couldn't afford it.

    b. My father got a promotion at his job, and we were able to travel to Europe.

I advise symbolically dividing the timeline into four vital stages (childhood, adolescence, youth and adulthood), that will organize you and can also give you a more specific framework, since in these stages we experience distinctive aspects of life.

When you detect an important milestone or experience, write the name of the experience (e.g., changing schools) and the age you were at that time.

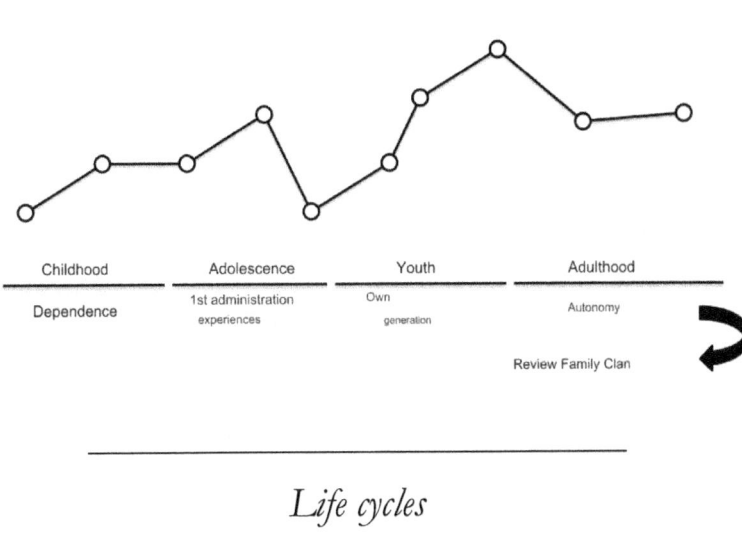

Life cycles

We have found some important distinctions to highlight, related to the four vital stages of the human being and its connection with money.

Childhood: It is a moment where we receive from the environment, we are dependent on others in every sense, we could say that at this stage we learn, in positive terms, to depend on others, we need to nourish ourselves. We are dependent.

Adolescence: It is a period where socially, biologically and perceptually, we search for our identity. We need to know who we are, and we do all kinds of experiments, in many cases risky, to achieve this. The adolescent needs to know "who they are." Many times, they pretend to "be an adult" to achieve it, using rebellion or obedience as clear flags. The search for identity governs this period. Independence begins.

Youth: It is a time of appropriation of one's own resources. In this phase, the "I can" flag is raised. We need to show ourselves that we can, we test our resources and knowledge. Here individuals usually start working, form a family, acquire assets, graduate from their university careers or consolidate their trade and activity. We are independent.

Adulthood: Although it is also a vital phase period, I like to present it as a subjective concept, which not all of us reach in maturational/perceptual terms. The adult is the one who is the owner of their own responsibility, they make decisions, take risks, and experience from a level of autonomy; always knowing that every act has its consequences, but they are the owner of their responses. This phase is governed by Autonomy. We learn to be interdependent, to value "we," instead of "you" or "I."

You might wonder: What does all this have to do with money?

The answer is that it has a strong connection and implication. Although we are already adults in biological and social terms, if we understand these four stages as maturational cycles (emotional-attitudinal), we could say: that we have dependent aspects (childhood), that we execute obedience or rebellion to find our identity (adolescent), that we have internal resources to show ourselves that "we can" (youth) and that we have a responsible part that takes care of itself (adult).

From these same places we can act based on money. There are people who live dependent on others in terms of \$\$ (childhood). Some manage money poorly or without responsibility, and in pursuit of identity, they do not measure any type of consequence (adolescence). Other people who really have acquired resources and begin to generate money on their own (youth), and finally, those who can direct money more responsibly, sensibly, being able to plan, measure and value efforts (adult).

$ Childhood	$ Adolescence	$ Youth	$ Adulthood
Dependency	Administrations	Own resources	Autonomy

Lack and abundance also go through these stages, since these germinate in gratitude and interdependence. In dependence or independence, one does not have a vision of everything that surrounds us, the interconnection with those around me privileges development.

Paying attention to how we respond to money is really interesting: Where are we today? Do we respond with dependency? Are we building our resources? Are we really autonomous and responsible?

Reminder: Responsibility = Ability to give answers

As a review, creating a timeline of the trajectory of money in your life, connecting it with these aspects, can offer important information to consequently detect many elements that allow you to see the meaning of money in your life.

Know your beliefs (danger)

$

We can enter from various points to analyze the issue of beliefs.

In itself, one of the meanings of the word beliefs is "to give credit," to trust something or someone. The curious thing about this is that we give super important credit and value to many beliefs that we have incorporated, whether cultural, academic or religious, without stopping to meditate and delve into their contents and foundations.

What I observed in myself and in others is that once a belief is established, whatever it may be, it works like a **criterion of truth for the person**; and the most relevant thing, as we already mentioned, is that they are not deepened by whoever owns them, it seems as if they provide criteria of identity and defend with tooth and nail. I have seen many make objective mistakes, with high material and psychological costs as a result of defending unfounded beliefs.

These unfounded beliefs become a rigid dogma, which can be questioned but not deepened, and that is where it becomes dangerous.

Imagine a belief regarding money that was "we can never save" (limiting beliefs). If this, which is a product, as we already know, of lived experiences (significance), is taken as unquestionable truth, we would be facing a complex problem, and consequently whoever defends this belief would never save money, by simple logic.

The wonderful thing about this is that I observe by contrast, how powerful the human being is when he stands firm with an idea, whether it is a belief or well-founded knowledge.
The impact of convergence that we defend as truth has on our reality shows the infinite power we have to create what we want.

There are limiting beliefs, which specifically prevent us from achieving what we want, and there are also enabling beliefs, which give functional direction to what we are looking for.

Let's define this 'word limiting' for our book: Do we see the limit? Is it written somewhere? Why do we impose limits on topics that have no limits? There is a physical human limit to running 100 meters, but athletes defy it. It is precisely when we challenge limits that we start to move forward. Many people with money like to say that first class on airplanes begins when the comfort zone ends. Comfort is tourist class, going further is first class. It is like this, the limit protects us, gives us security, a fence to move without difficulty. I continually see people talk about limiting beliefs, and just using that word makes the limits appear.

There are no limiting beliefs, they are just beliefs, surely born in the shelter of our affections to protect us from the uncertainty that exists beyond the limit.

It is important to detect both types of beliefs. Those that limit us, to redefine them, and those that enable us, to know them and use them as strengths. The first are based on our fears, and the second on our abilities. And in the middle of that balance are us and our decisions.

The fundamental thing in this issue is that we can be aware of what we decide. May the thoughts that govern our path be chosen as a result of a deep and sensible analysis, which always generate the well-being we seek.

Convert belief into knowledge. The process of appropriating an idea through one's own research generates knowledge with content. **And if knowledge is defended with tooth and nail, we will achieve everything we set ourselves to do.** Below, I share some of the limiting beliefs regarding the $ that we detected in the different seminars:

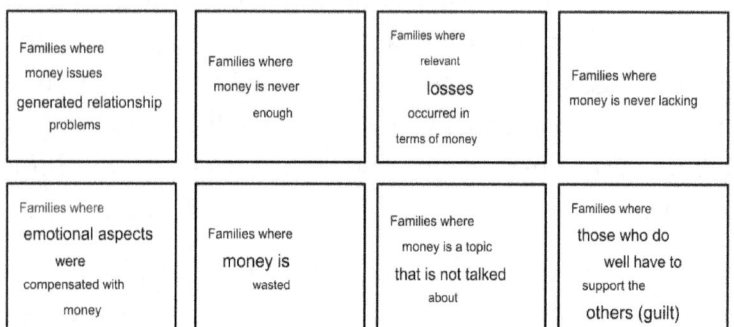

The important thing in this is to detect the mechanisms of thoughts (judgments) that we have, as we will see later, these blocks of thoughts generate neural networks, which send signals to our glands, generating endless hormones that end in behaviors. The habits we have in relation to money come from those neural networks (significance). The fact of consciously detecting and observing our habits, behaviors and beliefs in relation to money should help us say: Ahh, that's how it works! Recognizing ourselves in action with our poorly recorded habits will allow us in the future to free ourselves from "what **we believe** to be."

Finding the dinosaur doesn't change you

$

Seeking to understand

The capacity of the human being to be introspective, to think of himself as an individual and to observe himself "inward" is truly amazing, a mechanism that we take for granted, but if we stop to review what exactly happens, it is truly amazing what is presented as a possibility.

This ability to find causes, which generate effects, gives our logical faculty a wide margin of development and a unique potential, which we have been observing and verifying in the progress of civilizations and their scientific advances.

This type of scientific paradigm, "of finding the causes of creation and our behaviors" has had a strong impact on humanity for millennia.

The truth is that when the human being "understands" what is happening, through observation patterns that we have created or decoded to understand reality, we feel safer, more confident in ourselves for discovering the possible origin of what we study, being able to explain it and share it with others.

This is also the case with **soft** sciences, which include psychological and perceptual reviews of what we are living and experiencing. The different psychological and introspection currents have made a cult out of the "review of causes that condition us."

My take

I consider that searching for the causes is a very important step, but that alone is not enough.

Finding the causes allows us to recognize that the effects we experience have an origin, and that if I am experiencing something in my present that does not generate well-being, it is the product of a cause that can be solved.

For example: if I believe the reality that "I earn little money" (belief), surely if I found the cause I could redefine it, and by solving the cause, I will change my reality.

From my observation, this perspective is somewhat concise and linear since the specific change has several edges.

It is not enough to find the dinosaur (the causes). Beginning a path of introspection, an endless pit until you find the bones of it, does not guarantee that change will occur.

After accompanying transformation processes, I can say that introspection is a *very important attitude*, which if supported with determination, marks an anchoring point that allows a field of *appropriation in the person*. That is, the individual, that by going deeper, "takes charge," first of what they want to solve, and then of beginning a conscious path to understand, how and in what experiences, the beliefs that condition and create their reality were configured and introjected.

Finding "the dinosaur, (causes)" marks a positive and important attitude to go in search of what you want, **but in no way determines the arrival point, nor the achievement of what is being sought.** In other words, finding the dinosaur is only the first step that tests us if we are really worthy of everything we have left to learn.

Is introspection an essential step? We'll go a little deeper. It is important in the case that we have "mechanisms" that generate actions over and over again that we do not want to occur. At the same time,

I want to reinforce that if we take care of developing mechanisms that sustain desired results, they will completely destroy bad habits. **Simply put, in many circumstances, generating a new habit and "mechanism" simply makes the past obsolete, without the need to study it and return to it.**

Many times, I have been left "gloating" in the causes without being able to concretely change my reality.

I knew by heart the whys and wherefores of what I suffered, but my reality remained the same as before, and/or in some cases even more complicated.

Suggestion

Once we have identified the cause of some of our mechanisms, let's celebrate, but let's not stay there for too long; let's understand the why and what for of some of our traps, and let's stop making false turns, thinking that the solution lies in that cause.

We need to start building the new, open the channel to train ourselves with what we truly need to incorporate to change.

If I never received financial education, and I was taken by some limiting belief as a product of my life path; **solving my limiting belief would not**

empower me with money, it only disfigures the belief, and puts me in a position to begin training in financial knowledge, which until now I had not had the possibility of.

Many times, ignorance gets into the places where knowledge has not entered.

Going deeper into something is learning something new, it is not searching and understanding what was poorly learned.

The commands condition you. Have you already discovered them?

$

Take charge

Responsibility implies the ability to give answers. Depending on the type of responses I give to different circumstances, we could observe if I am really "taking charge" of my learning.

Although the first chapters give importance to the meaning we have given money, a product of different experiences that we have gone through, at this point in the "game," we need to stop taking refuge in our conditioning and face the true fears, those that expose us to the new, and leave the ghosts of the past for the movies, but not for our real lives; we will only change if we begin to navigate our own challenges.

Leaving behind cultural and family mandates is a sign of courage, responsibility and important ownership if we want to generate strong changes. Independence is the path we must travel before going to interdependence.

Instead of conditions, what we need to sign are agreements with ourselves, with the future we want to design, to venture into the uncomfortable, the risk of the new, the challenge of surprising ourselves in another, more prosperous reality.

Contrasts

The first thing we have to take is the reins of our life. There is no other solution, and stop blaming the environment, understand it instead. I observe that we all go through this situation every day.

Contrasts: Two different people but united by a past, with the same situations of frustration and pain (hard past).

- One of them does not change, justifying their entire life path based on the history they lived.
- The other decides that their future will be different and ventures into new ways of living.

The importance of some decisions projects us to change.

Think and remember, what valuable decisions have favored your life? Surely there are not many, but we can appreciate how a good decision opens a world of opportunities.

Lack and Abundance

$

Seeking growth

I always like to see soccer referees toss a coin to determine decisions at the beginning of the game. That constant rotation where the two sides of a coin are shown (heads and tail).

Does the same thing happen with lack and abundance? Are they two sides of the same coin? Is it a representation of the yin and yang of money?

Thinking that they are two sides of the same coin, or thinking about yin and yang, I establish that I would give the same "amount" of space to lack and abundance, and that is not the case. Having gratitude, by being a person who thinks of others and helps the common good with a look of interdependence (us) makes lack disappear and abundance increase. It's that easy, and that simple.

Living our life from lack is a way that we always have at hand, it is working from the "I" or the "you," from dependence or independence, but without thinking about "us."

A restaurant owner who only thinks about himself and his problems, and does not relate to his employees, diners and his service (the food, the purpose that unites everyone there) does not produce the oxygen necessary to breathe well.

Sometimes I explain abundance by sharing that the human being can breathe and stay alive with a minimum percentage of oxygen; but if that same person took a walk on the seashore, they would feel such intense oxygenation that not only would their lung capacity change, renewing their cells, but they would also have an experience of expansion and feeling of being loose, more abundant; it would undoubtedly modify your well-being, giving you the opportunity to think that there are different ways to breathe.

Two phrases to reflect on:

> "If the sea knew the fish in the fish tank, the glass would break even if it died." *Rafael Amor*

> "A bird that knows nothing but the bars, inside its cage thinks it flies." *Rafael Amor*

Without a doubt, when we discover new realities that expand us, we tend to repeat the good they generate for us.

Every experience of expansion in our lives is a record of abundance. Each opening towards the new, breaks known frameworks, breaks patterns, opening new possibilities.

Feeling abundant is an experience for each person; it always presents us with new experiences of learning, enjoyment and well-being.

Recording these indicators is a good way to begin to recognize some movements towards states of greater deservingness.

Abundance and *equilibrium*

Although abundance and lack are opposites, they are antonyms; from my point of view, they are actually two points, two stations that delimit a segment, that open the opportunity for a learning gap.

What makes a person more abundant is the presence of knowledge; those who do not have it will be more lacking in that subject and will limit their possibilities. I'm not just talking about technical or academic knowledge, I'm talking about knowledge that integrates all areas of the human being. He who has knowledge knows, he manages to achieve what he desires, he reaches his goals by taking action.

Regarding money, since we do not receive financial education, a large percentage of the world's population lives without some knowledge that would allow them to create possibilities to generate, save, invest and manage abundance.

Likewise, learning from books and seminars, if it were a way of incorporating knowledge, can be a trap if the assimilated learning is not implemented in practice. Many successful entrepreneurs have established themselves by practicing in reality through trial and error what they wanted to do and learn, without having to study great books and visit gurus on the subject.

There are no rigid recipes, but if the integration of financial education and the practice necessary to take action is achieved, a very assertive combo generally occurs on our horizons.

Likewise, and to leave a deeper image raised; abundance does not strictly have to do with money, although this is an important and necessary indicator. Abundance is directly related to **the equilibrium** that one generates between the expectations one has and reality (we will delve into it in part 4).

From this balance, which includes many decisions, quality of life arises, the feeling of happiness, which gravitates to four important pillars:

Physical life (biological), soul life (mental-emotional), spiritual life (transcendence), and financial life.

As a colleague says, life is like a chair with four legs, if they are not balanced, the chair wobbles, and one can fall. In reality, any of them that is not in balance with the other 3 produces a misalignment and a wobble, sometimes minimal, and sometimes more forceful. We can think of a chair where we sit, but we can also think of the 4 pivots of a house, of a table, of our life, of the 4 support points of a car... Will we be able to stop in time if a tire goes flat? Does going at crazy speed has a point, or is prudence a symbol of intelligence on a route? **Balance is key, and balance with our expectations is the key.**

And how do we figure out what the right expectations are? Well, I propose that you always have your expectations a little above reality, just a little, to always push ourselves upward, so as not to tempt us to stay still.

This conquest will depend on this balance; and to achieve this state we need to have the necessary ingredients (the four legs of the chair). As we are delving deeper into redefining the concept of money, we will give a particular focus in that direction, since it is an aspect where very little interest is placed in the quality of learning; but let us always remember to look at all the elements from above, from an eagle's vision. Let's never neglect a certain distance, **"the perspective"** of the important elements in life (the chair). Whether we are truly abundant will depend on it.

I have seen many successful entrepreneurs with poor lives, but I am also surrounded by people who have a lot of money and whose lives are abundant, rich in every sense; the latter tend to be a source of inspiration for those who want to grow. This is the proposal and invitation that we are reflecting on together.

I propose to take "eagle vision" and look at our chair (life) with perspective, where abundance sits.

Try to be honest in how you measure the percentages in the following table, being able to become aware of your current balance in life:

Priority	Physical Life (Biological Health)	Mental Life (Mental and emotional health)	Spiritual Life (Transcendent Sense)	Financial Life	
100%					
75%					
fifty%					
25%					

Mark with an X to manage the percentages.

This simple exercise will allow us to understand where we place our energy, where we direct our will and what interests we pursue as a priority.

In general, what we usually find in practice, when someone expresses that they are balanced, is the following table:

Priority	Physical Life (Biological Health)	Mental Life (Mental and emotional health)	Spiritual Life (Transcendent Sense)	Financial Life
100%				
75%				
fifty%	x	x		
25%			x	

We invite you to send us your responses to the editorial email netripublishers@gmail.com so that we can record the response metrics among readers.

When observing the indicators in the table, we see that financial life is not taken as something relevant, and although these people manage their economy, when we investigate this point, they usually share that their financial life is at the service of their basic costs to supply themselves, for their survival; that is, they do not prioritize financial life as something to improve, learn and/or channel. However, this type of balance sometimes tends to become complicated when financial life (which always exists) suffers a problem, unbalancing the remaining legs of the chair, breaking "the declared balance." I repeat, it is foolish not to give importance or mark the fourth column (financial life).

Let's get out of the internal traps and stop ignoring the obvious. Let's integrate all aspects to achieve full abundance.

Now, depending on the different moments in life, the life cycles and dreams of each person, the balance can be so diverse that it would be difficult for us to draw conclusions; but what I do want to establish is that we can always consider financial life in its measurements, only if we take it as something important, will we generate better maps of abundance, understanding that the resources that enable financial life can accompany and stabilize, reinforce and stimulate the goals of the other "legs" of the chair.

As **TONY ROBBINS** says in his book "*Money, dominate the game*": "we have to teach our mind to think that there is more than enough. We can leave scarcity behind and move toward a world of abundance."

Let's review the doing

$

Get in touch with your reality

As we shared in the introduction, in the first part of the book, we are focusing on the "review." And although we are analyzing the meaning frameworks of money, which lead us to redefine past experiences, it is important to focus on the PRESENT, and review our reality in the face of "Doing," and how we live day by day with that reality.

Many of the problems that we sometimes have are not necessarily associated with the past, they are connected to the "doing" of today. We are unaware of healthy habits that would make things much more fluid and dynamic, without the need to get entangled in old causes, which can even reinforce the mechanisms that we want to change.

So, ask yourself basic aspects of your financial reality today:

- Do you have a record of what your exact income is?

- Do you know what the flow of your expenses is like? Where does the money you spend go?

- Do your profits grow over time, are they static, do they have development plans?

- Do you have order, discipline and perseverance associated with your financial life?

- What is your context like, what habits do you have regarding money?

Reviewing these types of questions takes us to our reality, to what we are "doing" today regarding this issue. Only starting from reality can we solve something.

Just as there are ***dinosaurs (causes) of the past***, which condition us, there are also ***dinosaurs that take action***, which, if we do not take them into account, review and deepen them, we can also condition ourselves to fall into habits that do not take us where we really want.

Open a space in your log (notebook) to always review your ACTIONS, how we manage our strength in concrete terms. If taking action becomes practical and consistent, you will not doubt your progress, it will be a reality operating in your life.

Change your behaviors, inhabit new orbits, learn from other cultures, ask for new ways of doing, dare to travel different

paths and landscapes, give your brain new information inputs, challenge your actions as a fundamental part of your changes.

Sit down; take a deep breath, and take your reality today in your hands, feel it, study it, get to know it; dare to admit that there are habits that need improving, changing, relearning, projecting, in short, use enough energy to start *doing* with an innovative imprint.

"Change what you do, and your reality will surely change."

Synthesis 1

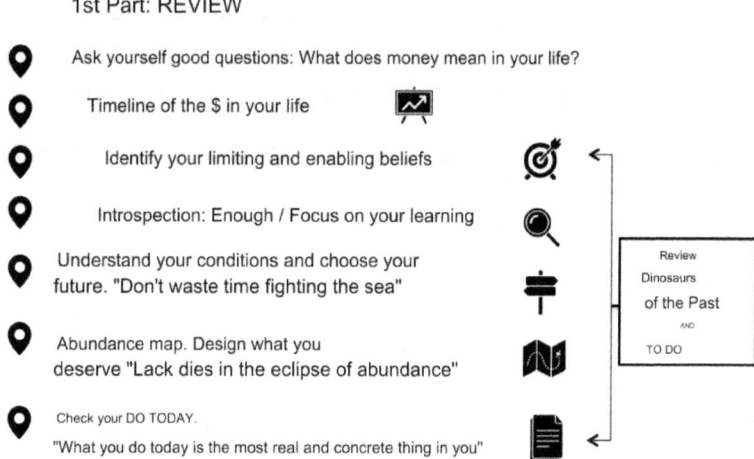

1st Part: REVIEW

- Ask yourself good questions: What does money mean in your life?
- Timeline of the $ in your life
- Identify your limiting and enabling beliefs
- Introspection: Enough / Focus on your learning
- Understand your conditions and choose your future. "Don't waste time fighting the sea"
- Abundance map. Design what you deserve "Lack dies in the eclipse of abundance"
- Check your DO TODAY. "What you do today is the most real and concrete thing in you"

Review Dinosaurs of the Past AND TO DO

In this first part we have concentrated on symbolizing our concepts of money, and why we are reading this book.

We learned that knowing the causes does not solve the problems, but it is our ACTIONS that solve them. To do this, we did exercises to understand the milestones of money in our stages of dependence (childhood), independence (adolescence and youth), and interdependence (maturity).

We review the appearance of lack and abundance, which, although they are opposite, does not mean that they have the same dimension in our lives, their impact is related to our capacity to GIVE and our gratitude.

Throughout the chapter we strengthened the concept of symbolizing and understanding our relationship with money, and mainly to stop saying that it is not important or that there are limits. They are just beliefs that are unraveled with healthy habits.

I invite you to reflect on part 1 before going to part 2 and write down the questions that appear in your notebook (log). Exercising is the muscle to develop habits.

PART 2

Take action!

Have a coffee with money

$

Ask it who it is

Joan Manuel Serrat (Spanish musician and poet), offers in one of his memorable songs a phrase that I want to highlight; "from time to time life drinks coffee with me."

Using this metaphor, I want to make an analogy and invite you to imagine what it would be like to have a coffee with what they call "money."

The one that uses so many clothes, that is sometimes fluid, that is sometimes scarce, the one that appears suddenly in some inheritance, the one that we receive as a product of a good negotiation, the one that is also offered in dribs and drabs until we achieve/buy something that we love so much... in short, who really is that character that represents so many forms and scenes? Why does it come to our reality? What will be its main function and purpose?

What answers come to your mind? Before moving forward, I invite you to take note…

What really is money?

"History"

In ancient times, prior to the existence of money, barter was the means by which the value attributed to the goods, objects and professions that were promoted at that time was exchanged. This system allowed for healthy compensation, in terms of each person's needs and what they had to give; obtaining a benefit and/or remuneration through another good, which in such situation was needed.

Over time, the development of barter became more complex and difficult. What objects have the most value? Is what they give me in exchange always what I need? Let's not believe that this question is from ancient times, there are people who ask it every day today in modern times.

The difficulties inherent in bartering led to the use of various goods to facilitate exchanges. These goods converted into general instruments of exchange gave rise to the first forms of money.

It is important to understand this concept of "exchange," since in the use of this medium something is always given and taken.

Nowadays, the use and specialization regarding money has developed profoundly. The global economic systems regulate, administer and manage the different gears, where "money" is the protagonist of a complex movie, where the results are not always beneficial in terms of the humanistic vision and the evolution of a global idea of supposed equity. And here it is not "money" that is responsible, this is just an indicator through which basic issues in the exchange with it are seen, where you can observe **what goods** are exchanged, **why** are they exchanged and **with what aim**.

Returning to the coffee / Value Indicator

Having coffee with the money, it answers me: "**I am an indicator of value, which encourages exchanges.** Many use me for that. When I balance the expectations of the parties, they are satisfied with my arrival. This is one of my main functions."

"In different countries I wear different clothes, but my function is the same. I am always available, many take me naturally, use me for altruistic purposes, others are afraid of me, some deny me, distrust me, others use me for fun and enjoyment, others bury me and hide me, others miss me like a Utopia…**I am always the** same… but I observe that people perceive me very differently and I only try to adapt to fulfill my role."

My purpose $$

"As for my purpose: I seek to generate an energy compensation, a compensation of needs; depending on the context, I change the value criterion, until those who exchange me agree on their benefits. When I became a bargaining chip, what they call "the supply and demand market" appeared and there I had to become more dynamic to compensate everyone. **But my purpose is to achieve compensation for the parties that exchange me.**"

Reflecting

As we see in this sincere and direct conversation with money, it manifests itself as having a specific and precise function and purpose. It does not have emotional issues that determine it, nor that give it identity. It is only there to fulfill its function and purpose.

With this I want to banish from the face of the earth that "money" is guilty of something, stop putting the responsibility on it! That medium of value and exchange is available, and **we are the only ones responsible for getting closer or further away from this good**, which allows so many possibilities in the world we live in.

I would spend hours listening to money describe itself, but without asking it I know that its life is accompanied by an altruistic goal, since it seeks the good of the parties even at the expense of one's own. Money seeks to satisfy those who receive it, but there it encounters an obstacle: accounting in everyday life is not always a balanced exercise. There are other elements of value in a transaction with money, trust, clear communication, favors, affection or detachment, and there is also greed, envy, and countless emotions, feelings, and sensations accompanying the transactions. We have seen all kinds of battles and wars over wanting to ingratiate ourselves with money, but at the end of the day, it is once again an indicator of value.

This is where I invite you to reflect on what the transactions of your life are, since they will be represented by a value. Although that chocolate that you keep in your pocket is today's most precious asset, since you are taking it as a gift to your child after a long day of work, remember that you cannot exchange it for a house, a car, or that child's school payment.

Emotionally, at this moment it may be worth more than anything in the world; money reminds us that everything has an indicator of value, which is a symbolization in a society.

Synthesis

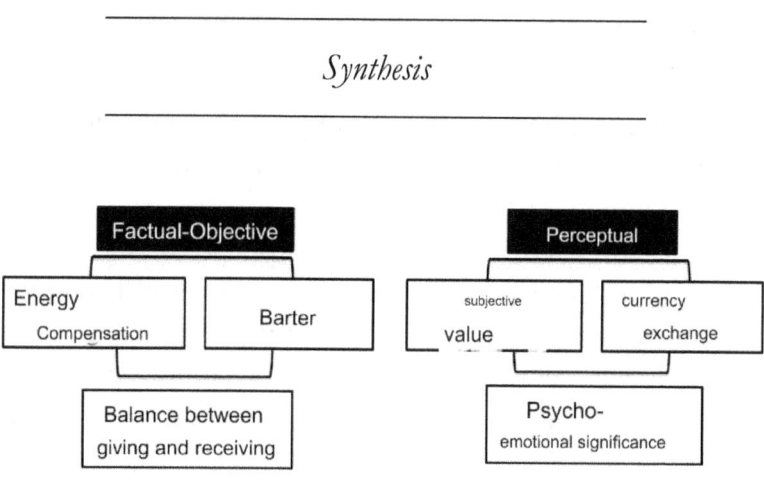

Unifying concepts that we have been developing, we could say that money has two aspects that determine it:

One clearly factual and objective, which contains its specific function and purpose, and another, a subjective aspect, which is determined by the meaning that each person gives it, based on the experiences they have had in their life.

It is important to stop at these points; the factual and objective, to begin to observe money as it is and feel worthy of its function and purpose; and the subjective aspect, to finish decoupling old beliefs and constructs, and start learning and applying new valuable knowledge to build a new future.

Some more history

Anatolian obsidian, used as raw material for the manufacture of tools in the Stone Age, was used as early as 12,000 BC. C. as a form of money.

Already in 9000 BC. C. both grain and livestock were used as money or as an element of barter (the first grain found is considered evidence of the date of pre-agricultural practices in 17,000 BC). The importance of grain with respect to the value of money is inherent in the language where the term for a small amount of gold was "grain of gold."

In the first cases of trade with money, the greater usefulness and reliability of the goods to be reused and exchanged again (their commercialization), determined their choice as an object of exchange. Thus, in agricultural societies, the goods necessary for the efficient and comfortable production of cereals were those that most easily acquired monetary significance in direct exchanges.

Societies were selecting some metals such as gold, silver and copper as optimal goods to function as money. These metals initially circulated by weight, in the form of nuggets, in fabrics and starch, in powder, etc.

History initially shows us how the goods that individuals developed circulated in terms of barter, and then with an object that represented said exchange value (money).

Dare to change

$

Value

Here is where I want to invite us to make ourselves uncomfortable, to try to jump into a new space, at first a little unknown, with other aromas, other textures, other scenarios.

Think about any change you have experienced, remember that vertigo of feeling excited and at the same time with adrenaline, tingling in your stomach, a certain dizziness, hope for the new, some sadness for what I let go, in short...**motion**. *Every important change is like an earthquake that shakes us, that awakens us, that often opens our eyes.*

I invite you to play, 'what would I like?'

Write what you would like to change in relation to your abundance (financial, spiritual, emotional, physical).

Honestly imagine what you dream of, write it, draw it, savor it, "render" it in various dimensions in your mind and in your feelings.

Now imagine that this image, that landscape of change is in front of you, but to get to it you have to cross a river. Now that you see it, would you like to venture out? Do you dare to get wet? Is it worth crossing the river? If the answer is Yes, welcome to the club.

Get ready to start moving like a child: "play, have fun and make mistakes," in pursuit of learning something.

We sometimes paint changes with drama, but deep down they are only learnings, and if **we decided** to learn, everything becomes much more pleasant; because challenges are seen as opportunities, as bridges to get to what I really want.

To encourage ourselves to change we need a "dream," a strong purpose. But to consolidate a change, we also need new knowledge, ideas that allow us to cross that river. Many times, the knowledge we have is not enough for the new. Perhaps you have not yet come across the precise keys that open the box of your abundance?

For now, focus on your dream, refine the image. What does it mean to sharpen the image? Imagine what you want to achieve, with details, as if it were a photograph. If you are looking for a business, imagine it; if you are looking for a change of job or role in your company, imagine; if you and your family are looking for a house, imagine it. Shortly we will review some knowledge that can help you achieve what you want.

As PETER DIAMANDIS says: "Abundance is not about providing everyone with a life of luxury, but a life of possibilities."

Change management

Managing a change can have two paths and ways of approaching it:

1. We change because life corners us, often with painful experiences and practically "forces" us to make learning journeys. Sometimes we change when we burn with our own difficulties. This change is intertwined with the verbs **survive and accept**.

2. We change because we decide to, because we see an opportunity for improvement and we can imagine it, dream it, project it and plan it. These types of changes bring much more enjoyment and motivation. Sometimes this change is intertwined with the verbs **grow and create**.

Both changes are real changes and allow us to go for new perspectives of life, to expand our perception, our vision. At the same time, they can be congruent, they can converge, like life itself, where black and white dissolve into gray.

Change number 1 is, as we said, more painful. Whenever we facilitate it, we like to facilitate it with the learning curve that grieving involves, because there are mechanisms that we usually apply to achieve change. Imagine a train that goes through different stations until it reaches a learning.

Change 1

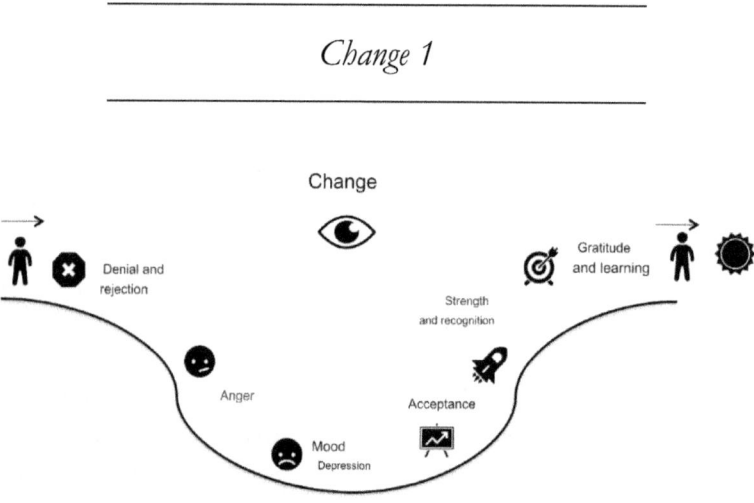

At first, when reality corners us, the first step is usually denial and rejection; we resist when we see reality, we reject what happens to us. As this instance remains, we begin another stage of anger, we become angry for not being able to overcome what is happening; then a significant low mood occurs, where the anger subsides, and feelings of fear and a certain depression appear. After this state, the sun begins to rise, the comforting sensation of real acceptance of what is happening emerges, it begins to feel like a rebirth, a new emotional balance that allows the possibility of learning.

An ally

In both paths we leave the comfort zone, our amygdala goes into action, our body releases cortisol, the stress hormone, fear appears, internal struggles begin in our body. This hormone is released into the blood and limits our expression and creativity, so here I advise you to have a must-have companion at all times: exercise.

Exercise not only takes care of one of the four legs of our chair (our biological health) but also reduces cortisol concentrations, and consequently, prepares us to develop better performance accompanied by internal (soul) and external (body) strength. The sweat we create when exercising repairs the bodily damage caused by stress and stimulates us, making us more alert, more creative, and healthier. I invite you to do simple exercise routines daily, which help us release residual stress that we cannot yet consciously manage. Having these allies is of high value for the adventure.

Change 2

When changing the second path, your approach is completely different. Here, by being a voluntary and directed movement, the stations of the train of change have another framework of action.

The first station is that of "dream," that of your purpose. This is no small task, identifying what I want to achieve.

The second station is to establish the "why" I want to change, what is the deep meaning that motivates me.

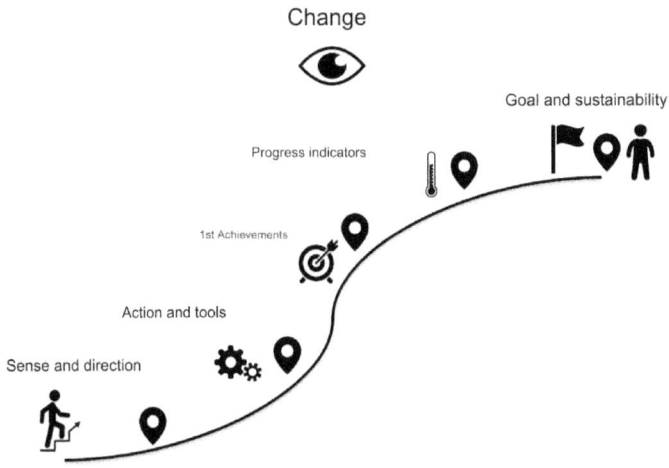

The third station consists of beginning to take concrete actions (mobilize) in pursuit of what you want.

Then in our fourth stage, we must progressively list gradual learning that allows us to learn the skills (tools) that we need for that journey.

On our path, as we have already made the first journeys, two more stations appear, the fifth station where we monitor progress (impact management), and the sixth, where we confirm the course to finish consolidating the change, our sustainability, which allows learning to be fixed in behavior as a habit.

Examples $$

On occasions, unpredictability or lack of knowledge causes a large debt acquired with a bank, and due to non-payment, a notice of seizure of assets is received. In these circumstances we tend to become alarmed, wake up and begin to understand that the learning point is imminent. If we can really cross the curve of seasons in the previous example (Change 1), perhaps we can resolve the urgency, but we cannot fundamentally resolve attitudinal and technical learning that will allow us to not experience pressures of this type again. **"It is key after storms and avalanches, to see what actions triggered it."**

It is different, when for example I want to buy a house; and one begins a planning process to achieve it (Change 2), carefully establishing the purpose and foundation of change, mobilizing ourselves to learn and measuring progress indicators, to end up obtaining the house that was planned.

Synthesis and reflection

We are always managing changes; life is a constant learning. What I want to highlight as important is that the decision and conviction of wanting to change is what makes the difference and makes us more protagonists of our actions. Managing with a certain direction makes us more responsible for our dreams, more deserving of our abundance.

Bridges to change

$

Change enablers

---

1. The first enabler that invites us to change is **knowledge.** Humanity in its evolution and progress is a chain of knowledge that was and is allowing us to find meaning in life and a logical and solid basis for any experience. Without knowledge we definitely could not evolve. Think about how knowledge enables you to solve problems that would be impossible without that resource. Knowledge opens doors and always will. This is my favorite ally.

2. **The affectivity**: our emotional life, the people who really appreciate us, want to see us grow, can understand our flight. These affective orbits are what reinforce our purposes, what push us to jump towards where we dream. They are there for the next step. Many times, we find them in our family members, in valued friends, and it also often happens that in work and professional environments someone sees our

talent and helps promote it. I still remember how a friend and colleague, in work experiences, trusted me more than I really trusted myself. He saw something that I had not yet grasped in myself, and I ventured with his encouragement and company to make me realize what he observed in the very vertigo of each experience. Experiences of extreme gratitude, which are lived when there are generous beings and when, on one's part, there is a desire to grow and take learning risks.

3. **Self-knowledge**: the work and inner cultivation that each person carries out in their internal world makes the questions and answers that unlock situations more effective. Dedicating time to inner care, to the assimilation of new knowledge will allow an effective enabler for change.

4. **Technology**: It is a result of the progress of the human being, a tool that allows us to solve everything from everyday issues to highly complex surgeries, it is one of the examples of the great creative capacity that the human being has. Since progress is so dynamic and rapid, in terms of time, it is important to update ourselves, as much as possible, with all the technologies that appear, seeing it as a tool that allows us to access the resource for which it was

created. In the past, to contact a client you had to send them a letter, and although now we miss the romantic aspect of it a little, we could not compare it with the assertiveness with which today we agree to contact people through emails and digital technologies. What is usually observed is that changes in technological paradigms usually generate initial resistance when using them. Like any change, it has logical resistance; what I want to highlight is that the good use of technology is a highly valuable enabler for many aspects of our daily work and financial activity.

The suggested phrase is: *"break paradigms, and you will find technologies to change."*

5. **Languages and cultures**: venturing to learn new languages allows you to incorporate other codes of perception. There are things that can only be described in one language and not another or can be described more accurately. Beyond handling several languages, what I want to express is that studying a language, even if one is not an expert, can make you live that perceptual experience of communicating with others and with yourself in a different way. The same thing happens when we travel, when we have the opportunity to get to know other cultures; we experience a change of location in

our perception that makes everything become different, and problematic situations in our daily lives become easy to solve if we took customs and behaviors from other cultures. Every trip I experience "opens my mind," I recreate a reset of my perception. After traveling I have made great decisions. It is clear that it is not the trip that changes us, but the fact that on the trip one gives oneself permission to open one's perception to the new.

6. **Art:** Fortunately, I always had this resource within my reach, thanks to my dear father, who gave me the opportunity to learn a musical instrument. I was able to go through different circumstances in the symbolic and powerful language that is inscribed in artistic expression. There I developed my creative world, and it was my second language to communicate. Music, painting, dance, theater, and any artistic expression allows an excellent enabler for change. Its subjective and tangible vibration makes it unique, leaving in each artistic work a symbolic manifestation for oneself and for others, it is another of the great resources of GIVING.

Your dreams suffer from inflation

$

Prioritize yourself

Yes, the truth is that in general terms, dreams suffer from inflation. Many people pursue dreams that are never achieved, the dream becomes a utopia, realities that perhaps others enjoy, but that apparently one does not feel worthy of having access to (you can read more about this topic known as Imposter Syndrome, term coined in 1978 by Pauline Rose Clance and Suzanne Ament Imes, which consists of a psychological phenomenon that makes those who suffer from it feel that they never rise to the occasion or that they are incapable of accepting that they deserve what they have obtained as fruit of their work. In Argentina and the Hispanic market, I recommend Ale Marcote's book "*How to transform imposter syndrome into your ally*").

Here, countless justifications appear in our mind, and as a result, one does not advance a single step in pursuit of our dream.

We have plenty of reasons to stay still, as we have already seen, dinosaur bones for life, but at this point, you have already claimed to be in the club, you have already focused on your abundance, and your feelings are already beginning to thirst for what new.

I'll tell you something else, sometimes we make dreams unattainable precisely to feel good about not being able to achieve them, after all they were impossible, right? Here I ask you to be careful, take short steps, climb a mountain one step at a time, you have to concentrate on movements that are easy to achieve. The sum of them will allow us to achieve unlikely goals.

Inflation

The concept of economic inflation is interesting. It happens when there is an existent **imbalance** between production and demand; this causes a continued rise in the prices of most products and services, and a loss of the value of money to be able to acquire or use them.

The same thing happens with your dreams. This is a good that one wants to acquire, but the resources I have are scarce to obtain it (knowledge and action). Many times, we tend to try to buy it with "printed money," money that is issued to balance a pressing situation, but in the long run it is fictitious money, which all it does is generate "bad debt," and distance the real possibility of what that we want to acquire.

Dreams are our products that increase in price over time, becoming almost a utopia, and our resources, our currency, our desire, which increasingly lose more value; and a labyrinth begins, a mirage, a circle with no exit, which generates debt, a debt with what I really want, with my goals of abundance.

Let's please get out of this lie and let's begin to take action, to produce with our own resources (knowledge, skills and desires), to trust that only in this way can we design our own trust, a currency of value, that allows us to build the bridge that takes us to our dreams.

Sometimes I am asked what the best investment is, how to overcome inflation rates, and sustain a significant rate of return, and the answer I give is always the same: **invest in yourselves**. When they create a product or service from their minds, they "make" it a reality, and produce value for others, when they "create" currency, they nullify inflation.

Let's get out of debt with ourselves. Let's learn new alternatives to value ourselves and achieve the abundance we deserve.

Interest is the measure of action

$

Doing

Everything that is important to us mobilizes our attention, captures our energy and focuses it, generating what we call interest. When something interests us, we feel attracted to it, magnetized to get closer to that reality.

This interest stimulates our will and allows us to TAKE ACTION, to get into movement.

The greater the attention, the more the activities we carry out increase. **That is why we say that interest is the measure of action.**

Interest has immense power and impact; it gives us encouragement; improves our relationships with those around us, family, friends, colleagues, neighbors, clients; it takes us out of this lethargy that inactivity produces in us; it expels us from the insistence on reflecting and thinking in an abusive way; reduces stress and fear; it drives us to explore new horizons and new relationships in life; supports the increase of skills; it makes us curious, the incredible seed of life itself; it leads us to read more, to walk more, to externalize and consolidate our purpose. I always say that our worst enemy is not reluctance, but indifference; it's not the loose of interest, it's the lack of it. If we are in a time of apathetic life, I invite you to think about small actions that boost interest in things, in people, too, and therefore this book, in finances, but mainly in GIVING. If anything shakes our interest, it is not just the ability to survive, but helping others.

Observe this mechanism; the energy we activate is always destined for our interests. Here it is essential to review ourselves since these guide us or not towards the abundance we are looking for. If we make our own interests and benefits coincide with the common good, with the interests and benefits of others, that is where abundance generates a robust, firm, unbreakable seed.

A question I see right now is: What can I give if I have nothing to offer right now? There is something that all human beings have in equal measure, some need more, and others less: time. Let's start sowing the seed of giving time, and we will reap spiritual, physical, emotional and financial wealth and abundance. What differentiates an action from an extraordinary event is simply an "extra," let's take at least a few seconds, minutes, hopefully more, to help a person every day we live. Interest is the measure of action.

Action and interests/financial life

A share in financial terms represents the ownership that a person has of a part of a company. That is, a possession asset. That action comes with rights and responsibilities, such as voting and dividends, but we will delve into this another time, nothing is coincidental, everything is part of a system.

Interest indicates both the cost of borrowing money from financial institutions and the profitability that savings or investment products offer us. In both cases we are talking about the price that one party charges for temporarily transferring its capital to the other, and here begins part of an undertaking, since we can impact those interest rates, which can be positive, neutral, or negative!

When we see an advertisement for a loan showing us the new car we can have, or the new repairs to the house we can make, or the trip we can take, or the push that the creatives have put to capture our attention, let us also remember that debts must be paid, and with interest! Let's think about how we can obtain and generate money, and perhaps we won't even need a loan to achieve it. This is the best financial education we can receive.

Of course, it is important to understand the accounting principle of double entry, sounds difficult, right? It is not. What I spend on one hand must come from another place. If I produce a sale of a product, then I get rid of an asset, it is the beginning of a transaction. If I buy something, then I get rid of the savings. But what if I don't have savings? Debts appear there, and if we have debts, we lose the shares we had.

Reflection

When I want to acquire a good, I need to generate the support (Money? Products? Services? Exchanges?) to obtain it... Isn't it curious that the financial term for possessing a good is called action? And that "interest" is that profitability that we can obtain when we own something? And that precisely the financial interest is always subject (measurement) to the value of the action?

This parallelism between human behavior and financial concepts marks a key to understanding the path of learning, not only technical concepts, but putting them into practice in an attitudinal way.

Continue reflecting on the phrase: **interest is the measure of action.**

Note:

I understand that when one buys an Apple share one seeks one's own interests, one's own benefit, but by acquiring that share we contribute to the common good that Apple produces in society, that is when the magic that allowed Apple to be the first company in history in exceeding a trillion-dollar valuation appears. Apple's energy flows through its shareholders, and the shareholders' energy contributes to Apple.

An indebted and sad trader somewhere in the world, by buying an Apple stock, not only receives the benefit of the share, dividends, growth in valuation, etc., but they are also energized, they also consider themselves part of a much greater whole, they are motivated, strengthened, empowered.

An example of our workshops

When there is a group activity, I call it the **magic of our time**, "that by thinking about the benefit of a "we," we benefit greatly individually.

The activation and impact that knowledge or a topic generates in a community is very powerful, since it allows us to deepen that knowledge from many perspectives and points of view, generating "the magic of the sea," that feeling of being unfathomable and strong when we are together learning something that interests us all.

In the workshops, when, for example, we bring up the topic of "managing abundance," like so many others, an exchange of information and experiences is generated, which allows not only to assimilate that topic, but also to deepen associated learning, weaving a larger framework than initially posed.

There you can see very clearly how our interests gain strength and action.

Design your new habits

$

Where we observe desire, process, discipline and habits there will be CONSISTENCY

Days ago, I was reflecting on the statement made by a client: "I can tell when a person is consistent because of the habits they have," he reaffirmed; "Someone who doesn't know their habits and doesn't improve them loses energy and is usually disordered."

Building a habit puts two fundamental aspects in motion, "process and discipline."

If you want to experience a process (progressive series of steps that reach a goal), review the content of this book several times. The only way to consolidate knowledge is by understanding that you have to plant it, water it, wait for it and watch it bloom. Enjoying the process in each season is a condition of abundance.

When I hear the word discipline, it seems a little harsh to me, it makes me cold to hear it. In the dictionary it refers to doctrine, especially moral matters. I like the word method better, doing in order.

That constant effort, whether willing or not, that we know builds, but that is difficult for us to incorporate.

Let's look at any high-performance athlete; I understand that not every day they love their sport and training from Monday to Monday, however, they know that step by step, it builds and perfects; effort that is later reflected in the smile of triumph when they achieve their achievements.

When I watch the Olympics, I get excited when athletes from different countries achieve their goals, an emotion that springs from me floods me almost with surprise, surely it must have happened to them; I manage to register that I feel identified with the effort that these athletes have made, put in 5 minutes of competition, in seconds in the 100 meters, in almost moments in some disciplines. It also amazes me that some know in advance that due to time and capacity, they will not come out first; but during the years of preparation, they train like a number 1.

These days, focused on writing this book to help develop growth in others, it happened that among other sporting milestones, the tennis player named Novak Djokovic won his twenty-third Grand Slam in the city of Paris, at the Roland Garros tournament, beating Rafael Nadal and Roger Federer, becoming the tennis player with the most Grand Slam tournaments; in that circumstance he said and I want to quote him: "You have to create your own destiny, live in the present and forget the past, believing in your own possibilities, because it is you who has your dreams in your hands." Djokovic himself expressly wanted to share that wish with everyone in his words of celebration.

Where we observe desire, process, methods and habits there will be CONSISTENCY.

When there is consistency and congruence, we feel confident, and we reflect the same towards others, we trust because we are prepared, because preparation gives us the dignity of the warrior, the result does not matter so much, I am 100%.

Always look for this energy, whatever you do, feel worthy, happy to do it, always try to be 100%. No matter how the equation turns out, you will always be "present," learning.

Returning to Money, many times you must have heard "John is financially solvent or consistent." Perhaps this observation includes in depth everything we have been discussing.

If we firmly want to start facing the issue of money with aplomb, we surely have to generate habits, which may require an effort at first, but later they will be our great allies.

Some important steps to establish habits:

1. **Clear purpose:** Let's imagine the goals. If they are small, let's have many, and if they are big, let's divide them into steps. The purpose and the reason for the seed.

2. **Short and medium term movements:** I return to the path to climb a mountain, let's think about the short steps (they will give us assiduity and continuation), and the intermediate goals (they will give us planning).

3. **Generate reminders:** use papers, post-its, whiteboards, computers, use your phone, but please, don't forget the commitments.

4. **Generate precise times:** Time is the same for everyone, let's be precise and mainly use time well. Be precise and responsible. Your time impacts the time of others. Don't be late for your appointments.

5. **Be rigorous (Not rigid)**: Rigorous is more related to being intense, not relaxed, whereas being rigid is linked to inflexibility. Be agile and flexible, intensely and accurately.

6. **Give yourself rewards for effort**: without rewards our body and mind begin to boycott us. It's like trying to exercise without the reward of hydrating afterwards. Here I want to quote a

businessman who once told me: "if you earn 100, reward yourself with 50, with half, do not be miserly with yourself, because money goes where it is rewarded." This statement is something to reflect on.

7. **Solve obstacles**: a problem is an unsolved question; fever is a consequence of an infection. Don't just stop at solving the problem, look for the roots that caused it.

8. **Find a friend in your will**: the will or desire to achieve something moves mountains, as popular sayings say. In the dictionary it is established as the power to decide and order one's own conduct. Its main adversary is procrastination, do not leave until tomorrow what you can do today.

9. **Record and evaluate the process**: I like the phrase "if we don't measure there is no progress." Since this book is aimed at the significance of money, I ask you a question: can you compare year after year if you have increased or decreased your capital (assets plus savings minus debts)?

10. **Learn to wait for the fruits:** Patience and prudence are friends of intelligence. Let's not be anxious, nor very relaxed. Taking advantage of the fact that the year of the publication of this

book the Michelin guide to restaurants in Argentina was established, we can use it as an example of not looking for a restaurant to be the best in the city in 2 months, nor do we wait 20 years for it to be.

The concept that it takes 21 days to form a habit comes from a study conducted in the 1950s by Dr. Maxwell Maltz, a plastic surgeon. However, more recent research has shown that the time required to form a habit can vary from person to person and depends on several factors, such as the complexity of the habit and consistency in practice. I like to add that in 21 days a habit is formed, with another 21 days it is reinforced, and after another 21 days we begin to sustain it easily, that is 63 days, almost 2 months. Let's start easy, let's try exercises. The first 21 days we do squats for 5 minutes, then the next 21 days for 10 minutes, and at the end on another 21 days we stabilize at 15 minutes.

These well-practiced steps inevitably lead you to build habits that trigger impacts on ALL your goals. We will need these 10 steps to start incorporating the knowledge that is in part 3 of this book.

What is important is uncomfortable

$

Make yourself uncomfortable

Who likes to be in uncomfortable situations? To my understanding, no one does.

The truth is that learning always includes a margin of discomfort. Everything that takes us out of our comfort zone is uncomfortable, it takes us out of our rest.

What is prudent to distinguish is that there are two types of discomfort:

1. **Discomfort towards the new**: When learning appears, I usually feel "pulled," a resistance to change that is natural and necessary to be able to learn. If, for example, I have never made an investment in a stock on the stock market, it is normal for me to feel uncomfortable venturing into it, but this discomfort has indicators of progress, that we are in search of something

more, I still remember my first investments in this sense. It was difficult for me to understand that without "effort" on my part my capital increased, opening the door to another possibility of generating money.

2. **Preserved discomfort:** it is presented differently; this happens when we need to "let go" of an old pattern, a situation, a job, a person, etc. A subtle discomfort appears that impacts your feeling, announcing that it is time to leave some space, to make a decision, to distance yourself. Taking time when this discomfort appears is advisable to determine if it is really this type. When we are right, respecting this internal call gives us relief, often preserving our integrity. Intuition also intervenes in these calls, making us uncomfortable, giving a strong message for us to act.

Surely when you read this type of discomfort, experiences that you have lived will appear, where respecting that call and leaving on time was necessary and positive.

The important thing

Prioritizing what really matters is not so simple, we could say that we tend to avoid many important things and focus on what is urgent. I return to the four pillars of abundance (spiritual, physical, emotional, and financial), we have already shared in previous chapters how decisive and important it is to attend to each of these areas, simultaneously and balanced.

We know that there are "important things" that are central, however we can get distracted and forget what is relevant.

It goes without saying that sometimes, when, for example, our health suffers a road bump, what is important immediately falls into place, it becomes a figure, and we can see this on more than one occasion.

Now, to voluntarily go to **what's important** you have to get uncomfortable, you have to display courage to resolve, boldness, channel and take one more step, one more step is always an indicator of abundance. Getting uncomfortable about what is important generates satisfaction that brings great well-being to the person who practices it. I invite you to make yourself uncomfortable about something important and you will feel what I am talking about.

Let's play **Mamushka** (or Matrioshka) where one doll has a smaller one inside, and so on.

1. Make a list of 5 important aspects in your life.

2. In each aspect point out 3 important points.
3. Add a relevant action to these 3 points.
4. Execute each action.
5. Then track how you feel.

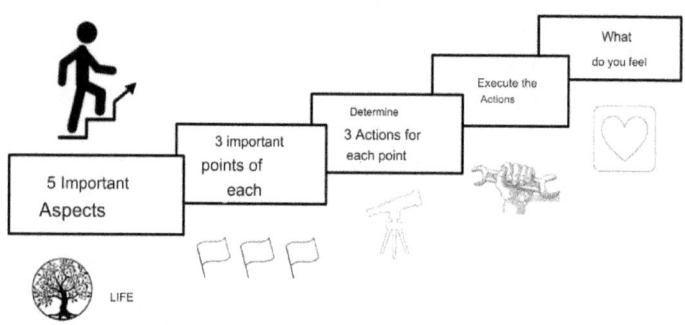

From 5 important aspects of life, 45 relevant actions arise.

Practice and you will feel congruence between what you set for yourself and what you do.

"Interest is the measure of action."

Mamushka

These dolls are an icon of Russian culture; they call them matryoshkas, but the terms Russian doll, mamushka and babushka are also used; whatever name you want to give them, these dolls are fascinating and are a Russian classic.

Today, there are several versions of these **dolls** which is basically "a doll inside a doll, inside another doll, and so on," you know them, right?

Much is said about their **meaning,** and one of the versions is that it was believed to be a symbol of joy, prosperity and wisdom, since when it is opened, it revealed what each person had inside and that was interpreted as a symbol of the inner representation of the people.

Other theories claim that **the mamushka means fertility and motherhood** due to the inheritance of his name.

What meaning do you want to give it?

Dare to think that the mamushkas are an invitation to delve deeper into what we are learning that each doll imprints a new state of knowledge, of strength, of the desire to move forward. Every time we move forward the doll becomes smaller, which suggests that we are simplifying (arriving at a synthesis), that each step implies a point of focus, of achievement in what we want to incorporate.

Emotional management

$

Your Cravings

We are spirited people. As some writings say, we have an anima, therefore we have a soul; a power plant, an internal engine that propels us in life, a traction that mobilizes the will towards our destinies, towards what we are developing as a purpose in our life.

I summarize a person's mood as the emotional management they can carry out of their internal world, of the combination of their thoughts, emotions and feelings that occur in their daily lives. Boredom, for example, is tiredness due to lack of that mood, and stress, we could say, is its disorder.

I understand that the state of mind is a result of the "emotional" management that each of us performs.

How do you manage your emotions?

Do you recognize the most dominant emotions in you?

Which of them do you feel harm you?

Which ones lead you to what you want?

From this management, that is, how you manage your emotions, you will be able to achieve what you want in balance with your inner state. If this does not happen, you can enter states of anxiety, which will disturb not only the management of your resources but may also affect your biological health.

Here, self-awareness, that is, the mastery of your internal states will be key so that you can achieve what you want, what you set for yourself, what you long for, what you want to see manifested in your life as a sign of abundance.

Anxiety

Days ago, I heard an analogy with emotional management that simply describes why we tend to enter daily states of chronic stress, sometimes without realizing it, and even in circumstances of well-being, we live stressed, fearful and nervous.

Example:

"It is very common and easy for a waiter in a restaurant to bring a cup of coffee to a costumer's table. But if that same waiter had to bring 40 coffees to one of the tables on the same tray, a simple task can become complex and very stressful."

This is what it is about, sometimes our daily stress comes from the accumulation of small tasks that, when combined at the same time, generate a voltage that, if not managed properly, can trigger an "anxiety crisis," anguish, an anger crisis, etc. Surplus energy will always seek to exit through some part of our biological system.

Our psyche has a space, an enclosure, so to speak, to contain the electromagnetic energy that our thoughts and our emotional world carry. Every responsibility, concern, purpose, always carries a volume of energy that must be managed, that must be learned to manage.

1. Something that usually helps me with this type of management is to prioritize my responsibilities, when doing this, perception begins to organize the course of will, so it attends the different points step by step, without running the risk of all the tension suddenly appearing to be channeled.

2. Another point of value that is usually a good resource, almost a way to oxygenate and provide objectivity, is to take "perspective of what is happening," almost as if it were happening to another person. I experience this resource daily when I receive consultants and clients with different problems, and in my

role as a consultant, I find a lot of assertiveness and objectivity to analyze different situations. This happens, not because I am a genius at it, but because I can take optimal distance and perspective from what is happening to my client.

This resource, when applied to oneself, provides a very effective key to get out of states of anxiety, and from there, we can begin to manage what is happening to us.

Another element of great value is our transcendent view of life, in our concept of abundance, our spiritual part. That feeling of internal fulfillment that we find when understanding and experiencing that creation and our evolution is much greater than what may be happening to us. Knowing that everything that is being presented invites us on a learning path. Even in circumstances where adversity seems to hit hard, as if God had become angry with us, there is deeper **reason** that invites us to move forward with serenity. Finding these states, which obviously require cultivation towards transcendent life, will allow us to go through and manage our internal states and the management of our energy with more consciousness.

I share with you an image of a staircase that randomly arrived on my cell phone just as I was writing this chapter, advertising tricks, perhaps of artificial intelligence, which I felt was a nice guide to manage our emotional management using some verbs.

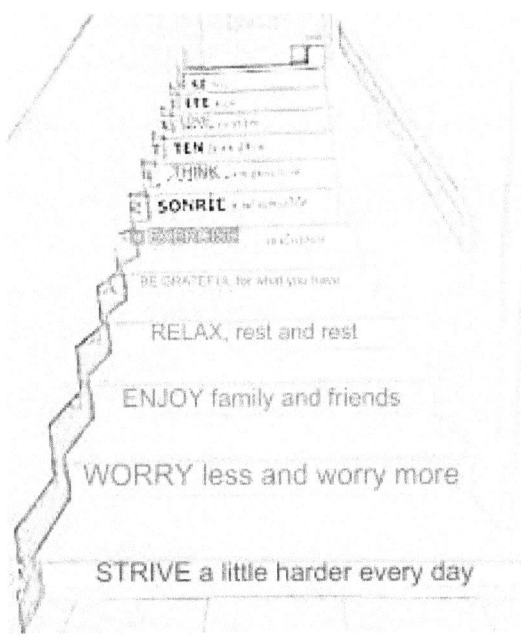

Another very interesting contribution from Tony Schwartz, which we use in our workshops and sessions, describes quadrants of how to manage our energy, amplifying moods and emotional states that allow more objectivity to review our actions.

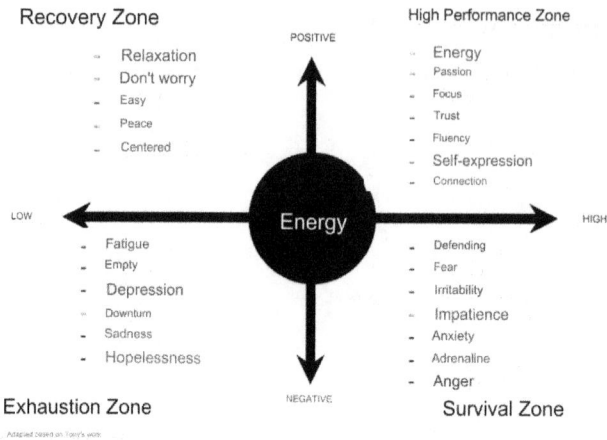

Try to review. In which area do you feel most identified? What are your most predominant moods? Which ones do you need to incorporate?

The administration of our energy is decisive for our emotional management to be healthy; only then will our actions be consistent over time.

Educate your mind and your heart

$

The three brains

The advances that neuroscience and quantum physics have developed in this regard are notable, being able to explain the relevance of mental life in human beings; the impact of thoughts, generating emotions, activating glands that release hormones, evidencing palpable behaviors that started from an idea, a mental spark (thought) that triggers our experiences.

I stop to reference Paul MacLean, an American doctor and neuroscientist who made important contributions in psychology and psychiatry. His evolutionary theory of the triune brain proposes that the human brain is actually three brains in one: the reptilian, the limbic system, and the neocortex. Joe Dispenza, American international speaker, Doctor of Chiropractic and writer, gave more content to the topic, exploring how the brain learns, how it processes information, and how, when not stimulated by new experiences, becomes addicted to patterns of comfortable and repetitive behaviors.

I will try very briefly to explain some mechanisms that will allow us to understand how to educate the mind and heart for what we long for.

The importance of understanding that we have 3 brains will help us educationally and practically in the way we process the information we receive consciously and unconsciously.

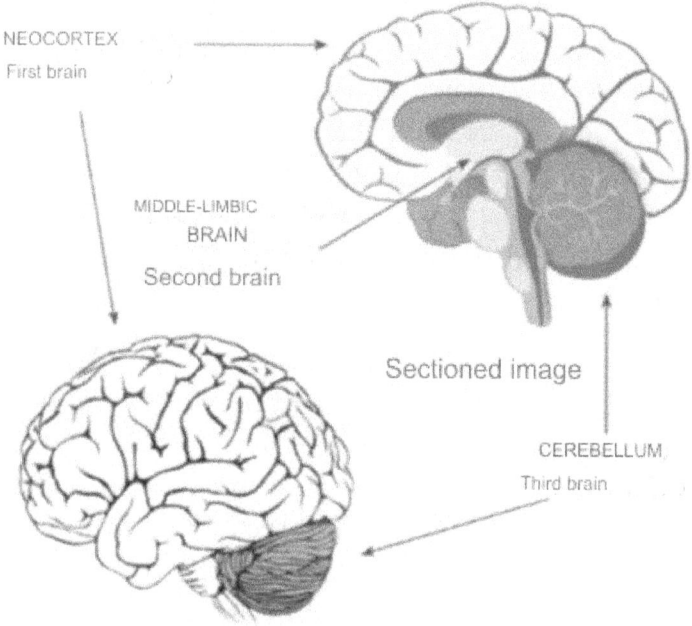

Graphic from the book "Stop Being You" by Joe Dispenza.

The three brains, as the graph describes, are what allow us not only to incorporate knowledge, but also give way to it by acting with it, experiencing what we incorporate, and in this experience, it generates habits that, once installed, begin to respond spontaneously in our behaviors.

The example that I usually explain when I touch on this point is "riding a bicycle."

Initially, when we learn, we use our *neocortex brain* to understand, reason and project "how to ride a bicycle." Once incorporated, once I understand what to do, I practice, using the *limbic brain,* we experience through the physical senses and we have the experience of "feeling" what happens to us when we "ride a bike" (if it is pleasant, if it scares me, if it is fun, etc.). Everything that refers to feeling (sensory and subjective) is taken by this brain. Therefore, what we enter through the *Cortex* brain, we experience it with the limbic brain. If I experience the experience of riding a bicycle repeatedly with the same sensations, I generate emotions, and once this action is repeated for a long enough time, becoming a habit, this is where the third brain, *the cerebellum*, generates what is understood as "automatism," an automatic reaction or response to assimilated knowledge; and in this way, once we have achieved that knowledge in our *cerebellum*, it acts spontaneously, without the need for our thinking and senses to intervene.

The example shows it clearly, when we spend many years without riding a bicycle, one gets on and without thinking about it, pedals off, as if time had not passed. This experience simply points out highly complex processes that these three brains manage.

I highlight this mechanism, because just as we record valuable knowledge in our cerebellum, we also tend to assimilate knowledge that does not lead us to achieve what we want. Our brain does not identify or distinguish between good and bad; it is only faithful to its mechanism of how to record knowledge and habits that we usually repeat.

If, for example, I learn to park my car incorrectly, using the mirrors incorrectly, calculating distances incorrectly, and that "error" or lack of precise knowledge, I do not incorporate correctly, and I continue parking "as I can," it is very likely that this "as I can" gets engraved over time in our *cerebellum*, and when parking, respond poorly to that act.

Let us reflect that in this way we have recorded knowledge that leads us to be assertive and others that generate precisely the opposite. When in the first chapters we talked about beliefs (blocks of thoughts) that are incorporated, it is because we have gone through experiences with them and today when it comes to acting, they respond automatically, without the intervention of our reasoning and consciousness.

Therefore, educating or re-educating the mind and heart (emotion-body) is totally necessary to learn any valuable approach.

In relation to money, let's think that we surely have many "incorporated automatisms," many ways of responding that are already learned, some leading us to assertive points (abundance) and others generating lack mechanisms over and over again.

The interesting thing about neuroscience is that it is scientifically demonstrated how neural circuits generate traces that we repeat over and over again and that we have the habit of reiterating them.

So, it will be important to know that if we want to incorporate something new, we will have a kind of internal battle; between what I want to learn and what I need to unlearn.

When incorporating the knowledge that we will provide in this book, it will be essential, if we want them to co-invest in a concrete reality, to understand them, practice them, experience them, and in this way by repeating them over time, a new habit and mechanisms is "reimplanted" in our *cerebellum*. When that happens, we could say that we are changing voluntarily, consciously.

I firmly invite you to confirm that we can change, that we can incorporate new ways of **doing and being**; it will all depend on our desire to improve ourselves and open ourselves to breaking the molds, the structures, that we understood as our own and that now, due to the desire to improve ourselves, require comprehensive re-education.

The three brains and $$$

Let's imagine how these 3 brains would work for our goal with money. Understanding our inner laboratory will give us the opportunity to create and record our learning.

The first thing we have to understand is that we harbor poorly recorded habits in the cerebellum, which will seek to continue acting automatically.

For example, "if I never write down my income and expenses" and this is recorded as a habit, we will have the inertial recurrence of not writing down our money flow. Just because you understand doesn't mean that something stops happening. The good thing about all this is that we also know that when we give our brain the information and experience that writing down income and expenses is beneficial for our financial life, it will banish the old mechanism, being able to change behavior and found a new habit.

For our brain to understand this new signal as good for us, we will first need to have new knowledge, and to do this we will have to use our first brain (neocortex) to understand this knowledge well (for example, why and how to write down the flow. When we find new knowledge useful and meaningful, our brain screams "I understand").

Now, for our brain to understand that this is beneficial, we will have to put this knowledge into practice. When the limbic brain (2nd brain) begins to feel new and pleasant sensations through the physical senses, it finds a different input and this new behavior takes shape. If we can sustain this experience and sensations for a reasonable amount of time, this behavior is recorded in the cerebellum as an active habit, banishing previous behaviors.

This is our processor, very similar and superior to that of any computer. The interesting thing to note is that we know more about how our notebooks work than about our own celestial and biological machine.

We have within us the best of laboratories to generate almost everything we set out to do, always using the rules and limits of the process, we have free autonomy to create and be masters of our destiny.

Assuming this possibility is a great thing. I still remember when I started to experience changes in relation to money with this perspective and responsibility.

The interesting thing was not only that I could incorporate new behaviors and knowledge, but I could also perceive that I was doing it consciously, that is, being fully aware that I was working with my inner laboratory.

That feeling of self-control generated a before and an after. From there "I took on more dreams," knowing that I had the most important tool to achieve it, my own laboratory.

Synthesis 2

2nd Part: ACTION

- Understand what Money objectively is. Coffee with $
- Discover your strength and start the process of change
- Determine your dreams, acquire the tools to move towards them
- Discover your interests and take action, that's where your energy goes
- Design your habits, choose and plan how you want to live
- Look for what is important in you, even if it is uncomfortable, you will save time, resources, inconveniences; it will be simpler
- Understand your internal mechanisms, from your inner laboratory, create your future

We begin part 2 of this book by having coffee with money and symbolizing the measurement of implicit value. At the same time, we begin to encourage ourselves to change, to improve, to take action, the opposite of lethargy and apathy.

We understood that dreams can be overwhelmed by "inflation," and that "interest" is the key to the growth of our capital.

Above all, we begin to understand that action makes sense if it is accompanied by strengthening a habit, which will last over time.

It is no use thinking that by splashing around in the water we will produce a permanent change, and "wanting" alone is not enough. Discomfort is our ally because it expels us from erroneous learning (limiting beliefs) and encourages us to explore new destinations.

PART 3

Learn!

Financial education

$

At last

All education starts from a need and aims at a goal.

I highlight the point of need, because that is how civilizations have progressed, based on the needs that they were identifying to satisfy, different models of education were developed.

With respect to financial education, it is an almost unexplored terrain in the world's population. Some advances have occurred based on the globalization of information in recent decades, but there is still no comprehensive approach that contemplates the range that we try to cover in this book; where not only technical issues are addressed, but it is necessary to review how this converges in the different aspects of a person's life, individually and collectively.

This book focuses on some points that I consider necessary to start sharing so that you fully understand what it means to have a good financial education.

This initially lies in starting to have a common language that can be understood in a simple way. Always speaking in the same language energizes and facilitates understanding in any learning. Therefore, it is necessary to handle some ABC concepts to be able to follow the common thread of basic and more complex ideas.

Another factor is that the knowledge learned serves first for the individual contribution of each person, and then to contribute to others, being able to generate a virtuous learning feedback loop.

An aspect that I consider distinctive is the emphasis we give in this book to the central section of the significance of money in personal, relational and cultural life. The significance and psychology of money is a determining factor in the changes that we can incorporate in this sense.

A comprehensive education must also have a wide margin of contextual adaptation. When, how, where, who is trained and for what specific goals will be highly relevant for learning to take the intended direction.

In this book we try to inaugurate a new way of approaching this topic, allowing the points that we are highlighting to be articulated with each other, allowing the reader who tries to assimilate learning, to interpret for themselves the valuable content that they need today, progressively and based on their experimentation, they will take greater interest in delving into other contents and scopes.

Basic concepts to keep in mind

We share some basic concepts that will allow us to homogenize language and some content that will be developed in the following chapters:

Budget: A budget is a financial plan that details your income and expenses. It helps you have clear control of your money and allocate your resources effectively. Planning is the opposite of \improvisation; plan and you will observe better performance and well-being.

Saving: Saving is the practice of reserving a portion of your income for future uses. It's important to save regularly to build an emergency fund and to achieve long-term financial goals. Some people call it the "own bank," its own entity that also finances dreams.

Debt: Debt is money you owe another person or entity. It can be in the form of student loans, mortgages, credit cards, etc. It is essential to manage debt responsibly and pay it on time to avoid accumulated interest.

Interests: Interest is the additional costs associated with taking out a loan or leaving money in a savings or investment account. It can be interest paid (when you take out a loan) or interest earned (when you have a savings or investment account).

Investment: Investment involves using money to acquire assets with the goal of long-term gains or returns. Investments can be stocks, bonds, real estate, mutual funds, among others. Some indices are S&P 500, Dow Jones Industrial, Vanguard 500, etc.

Diversification: Diversification involves spreading your investments across different asset classes and sectors to reduce risk. By diversifying, you avoid putting all your eggs in one basket and protect yourself from significant losses if an investment doesn't work out as you expected.

Inflation: Inflation is the sustained and general increase in the price level of goods and services in an economy. Inflation reduces the purchasing power of money over time, meaning the same money buys less in the future. I want you to compare it with another when you observe inflation in one currency. Perhaps the Argentine peso depreciates, but it has another relationship against the dollar and/or euro.

Risk and reward: There is a relationship between risk and reward in investments. Generally, riskier investments have the potential to generate higher returns, but also involve a greater risk of loss. It is important to understand your risk tolerance when making investment decisions.

Emergency fund: An emergency fund is savings set aside to cover unforeseen expenses, such as job loss, emergency repairs, or unexpected medical expenses. It is recommended to have three to six months of basic expenses in an emergency fund.

Financial education: Financial education is the process of acquiring knowledge and skills related to money management, decision making, and planning to achieve goals. A solid financial education is essential to making informed decisions and having a healthy financial life.

Stock Exchange: It is an organized market where financial securities, such as stocks, bonds, options and other instruments, are bought and sold.

Actions: They are titles representing ownership in a company. By purchasing shares, you become a shareholder and have the right to participate in the company's profits and decisions.

Stock indices: are indicators that represent the general performance of a set of shares on the stock market. Some famous examples are the Dow Jones Industrial Average (DJIA) in the United States, the S&P 500 and the NASDAQ Composite.

Volatility: is the measure of the variability of asset prices on the stock market. High volatility implies larger and faster fluctuations in prices, while low volatility indicates more stable movements.

Performance: is the profit or loss obtained from an investment in the stock market. It is usually expressed as a percentage and can be positive or negative.

Dividends: are periodic payments that a company makes to its shareholders as part of distributable profits. Dividends are a way to earn a return on stocks.

Broker: is an intermediary that facilitates the purchase and sale of securities on the stock market. Stockbrokers can be individuals or companies and are authorized to carry out transactions on behalf of investors.

Technical analysis: It is an analysis approach that is based on the study of historical asset price patterns and trends to predict future market movements.

Fundamental analysis: is an analysis approach that evaluates the financial health and performance of a company to determine its intrinsic value and make investment decisions.

Purchase order and sales order: are instructions given to a stockbroker to buy or sell a particular value. A buy order is used to purchase a value, while a sell order is used to dispose of a value.

Risk: In the context of the stock market, risk refers to the possibility of financial loss. All stock market investments carry some level of risk, and it is important to understand and manage risk according to your tolerance and financial goals.

The four ways of living

$

Money Flow

Of the various well-known authors who write and advise about money, I tend to share Robert Kiyosaki's concept of the money flow quadrants (from his books "Rich Dad Poor Dad" and "The Money Flow Quadrant").

He proposes four ways to position yourself within the flow of money. What I want to highlight is the integrative and beneficial aspect that I have been developing with the different cases in which I accompany, where I put emphasis on the way of living each of these quadrants, without rigidifying or judging each of them as good or bad.

QUADRANT OF MONEY FLOW

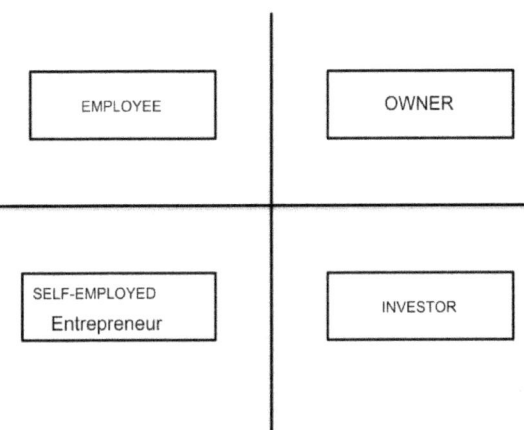

In practical experience I have found an integrative way to learn the importance of each quadrant and be able to adapt it to each circumstance we experience to find our objective benefit according to our needs.

Four ways to live: the life of an **"Employee"** who is paid for their skills, for the scope established for them and who at the end of the month receives a salary for their contribution to the organization where they "work." The type of employee segment is very broad, but the concept I want to show is that employees work for a boss, for an owner. The latter is the one who really takes all the company's profit, responsible for the successes and failures. He is also the one who absorbs the risks.

Another way of living is that of an **"Entrepreneur,"** who decides to take action and "work on what they like." Many times, they begin as entrepreneurs and end up as businessmen, which entails many maturation steps in professional, personal and organizational terms. Many employees at some point in their lives decide to become entrepreneurs, trying to unify into their work life what they like to do for themselves. I have accompanied many cases of these processes, a topic that has several aspects to delve into; but let's keep moving forward...

Another way of living is that of **"Owner,"** Kiyosaki calls it the life of the Rich, which obviously also has its costs in emotional terms and responsibilities, but it is true that the owner, if he really is an "owner," is the one who can treasure the concentration of all the efforts towards his pocket.

The remaining quadrant is the **"Investor,"** they are strategic and objective, accurately calculate the concept of profit, and also know how to analyze risk indicators well, from which they manage their decisions when investing, with the confidence of increasing their assets.

The quadrants have a particular "DNA" and a purpose that defines them, which makes us move according to the different ways of living according to the chosen quadrant.

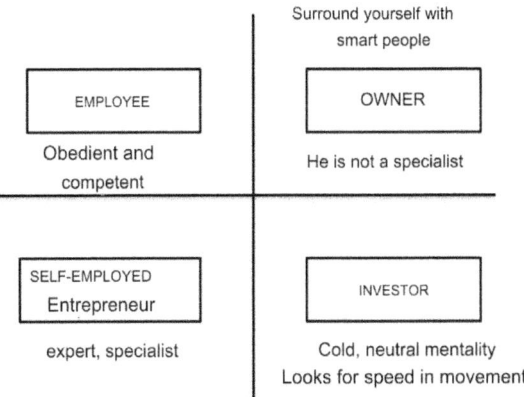

The **employee** wants to be paid for their skills, that is their purpose, many have a lot of money in their career plan if they manage to "sell" their skills well.

The purpose and motivation of the **entrepreneur** is being an expert and specialist in what they do, this aspect in most cases has a strong emotional aspect, which makes them "fall in love" with what they do, giving them, on one hand, a unique and committed "push," but in some cases, also limit their growth. I call it "the craftsman's disease." They put so much affection into the product they generated that later, emotionally, it is difficult for them to sell it, as if they had become attached to the product made. These limiting beliefs must be worked on so that the entrepreneur does not become trapped in their own narcissism of entrepreneurship.

The purpose of life of the **investor** is to obtain assets based on their technical expertise in the investment strategy, whatever the investment, a mature investor always has a "clear head" that objectively analyzes the return on their investment. A cool mind is one of their decision-making talents.

The **owner** is the number 10 of the team (midfielders), they know and manage the players around them. Sometimes they are not the one who know the most, but they surround themselves and hire the best experts. They know that some efforts are made by others, and that their strategic mind is what determines their DNA and their achievement when it comes to managing and earning money.

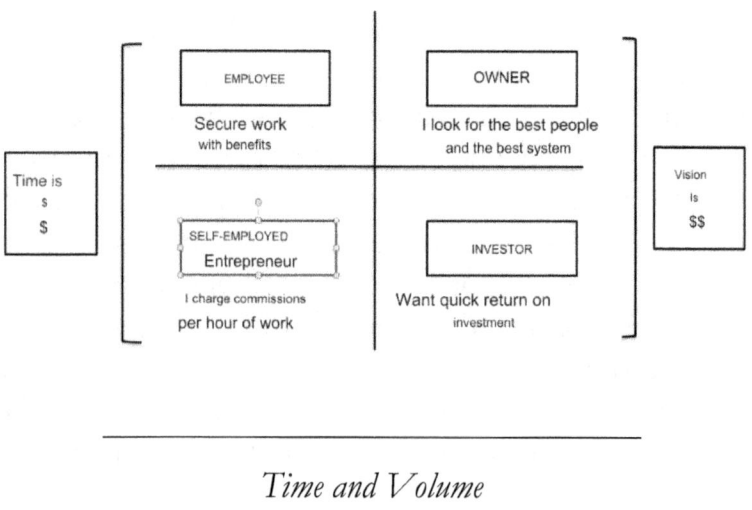

Time and Volume

Both**, the employee** (safe work with benefits) and **the entrepreneur** (charges commissions for what they like to do) are subject to the "labor," to the hours of work that they can perform. In both cases, the ability to manage time is key, they make money over time; this is where the phrase "time is money" fits like a glove. That is, the amount of money they can earn is closely related to the unit of time they have to dedicate to the tasks they perform.

Meanwhile, **the owner** (look for the best people and system) and **the investor** (objective mind), have a different equation of time. What regulates profits for them is the volume, it is not subject to one's own capacity since those who produce are others. In the case of the owner, they hire employees and or systems to generate volume of products and make more profits, and thus become richer. In the case of the investor, if they invest, for example, in shares, they get on and are part of "a moving train" of established companies, and only by contributing their assets they receive profitability, but the production time is also done by others, it does not depend on the investor. **This is one of the formulas of wealth.**

Days ago, an image came to me in relation to wealth: "Do not invest time in producing rain (liquidity), but rather, invest in good "buckets" (containers), so that when the rain reaches the ground, you can treasure it."

```
┌─────────┐     ┌─────────┐
│ Time is │     │ Vision  │
│    $    │     │   Is    │
│    $    │     │   $$    │
└─────────┘     └─────────┘
```

So, we have two paradigms: "Time is money" and "Volume is money." One subject to **time** in producing and another oriented to strategic **vision** in how to generate volume.

The Rich have transformed "seeing" into "vision." They develop an optimal distance with what they manage, which allows them to play as a midfielder, the number (10) of the team.

Integration

I want to highlight the importance of understanding that none of the quadrants is better than another. **And they can also all come together in a person's life.** Although those who manage volume look more "apparently rich," each quadrant has its strength and weakness, its cost and its benefit.

I explore these quadrants as learning possibilities in each of their forms. We have to practice learning flexibility to incorporate the 4 quadrants into our lives. Let us remember that the choice of each of them depends on the concept of balance (abundance regulator) that we have between our reality and the expectations that we direct for our present and future.

Therefore, let's begin to understand more deeply the talents of each quadrant; since what marks the point of assertiveness is often determined by the circumstances in reality itself. Certain contexts may require me to "be an employee" (security in knowledge), "be an entrepreneur" (personal expertise), "be an investor" (objective and assertive mind) or be an owner (strategic vision).

"Assertiveness depends on which quadrant I apply, based on each circumstance." It is key to understand that what makes knowledge reach its point of effectiveness is to "read" the environments and circumstances well and have the proper "tact" to achieve its application.

Emotional thermometer

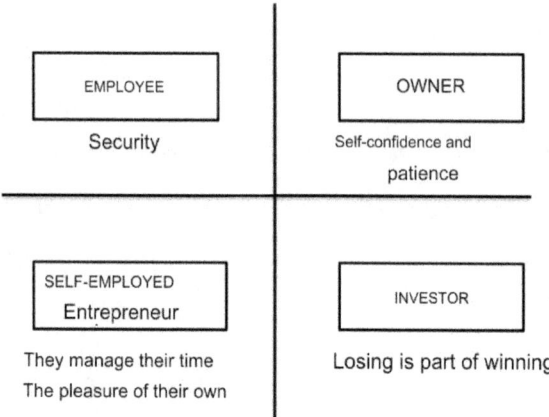

To provide more resources to learn about these ways of living, I share elements that we have developed in practice and in research.

These quadrants are also moved by emotional benefits, and mental life is decisive in our decisions and behaviors. The employee seeks "security" when they are hired with stable scope and benefits. The entrepreneur seeks "freedom" in managing their time as they please and also the benefit of feeling responsible for "their own things." The investor finds emotional stability when they understand that the risks they run are part of the game. The risk is high, but their expertise and objective mind moderate and stabilize. The owner seeks to feel that they can direct and manage more complex systems, they search in emotional terms, **thinking big** when developing confidence and improvement.

Practice

Write down in your log in which quadrant you live most predominantly today.

- Search within yourself, which quadrant would you need to incorporate into your life?
- Do any of the quadrants feel very foreign to you?
- If you find one, justify your answer.
- Of the quadrants that you don't know, does any value judgment come to mind?
- What comes to your mind or your feelings when you hear: Employee – Entrepreneur – Investor – Owner?
- Write down resonances, we will use them in the methodology.

The four keys of a rich man

$

Attention

Within the consulting Hallway firm (leader in finance), where I collaborate with the team in the training area, we are developing four keys that open a world when analyzing personal and organizational finances. A scheme that allows us to discern areas that we need to incorporate and balance to have financial health.

We have realized that there are four areas that come into play when analyzing our finances. We have placed them in 4 squares, and in this chapter, we will delve into their characteristics and operation.

It will be interesting to review in each one what aspect we can incorporate and/or renew from the following description.

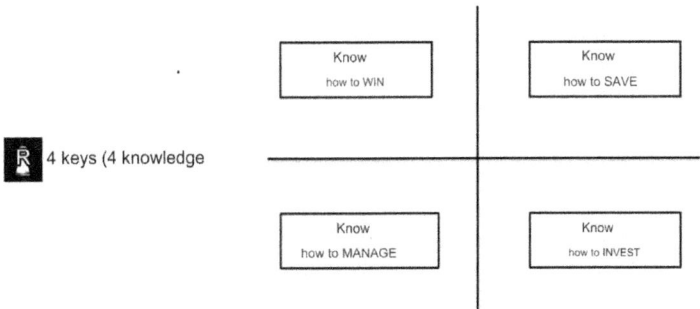

Each of these keys (WIN, SAVE, MANAGE, INVEST) has specific knowledge, and their combination generates the dynamic balance that we want to share according to the goal we have in front of us.

We have seen in some cases that some people know how to make money, like second nature, but perhaps they are deficient in saving or managing. Others manage very well, but it is difficult for them to get out of the restrictive administration, they cannot generate new income curves. In other cases, they earn, manage and save very well, but have no idea how to invest money.

We share the following chart so that you can scan yourselves and see with the naked eye, what is my strong aspect? And what key do I need to add more quickly?

Concepts	Enter your priority
Gain	
Save	
Manage	
Invest	

Mark with a 1 the aspect that you most need to incorporate into your financial life; you can use 2,3 and 4, always knowing that 1 is the highest priority and 4 is the lowest priority.

Our financial health will depend on this balance, as we said.

(Key) Know how to win

The great desideratum that we all want to conquer. What I do want to clarify is that knowing how to win involves the rest of the quadrants, since their appropriation always generates assets in growth. But referring specifically to this quadrant (knowing how to win) I want to provide some valuable goals that can help open the door.

Knowing how to win is based on the possibility of "generating," of giving a value that is rewarded; that is why the phrase "if you want to win, value yourself higher" often appears. It is proven that valuable content that is offered in the right context is always rewarded; that is, it is paid.

First question to ask ourselves is:

What do I have of value to give? In what area do I feel talented, useful? What assimilated skills can I provide? What things do I do that can be a source of value?

Answering these questions is of great importance, since if we manage to detect what our contribution is, our value, we already have a fundamental point to start.

With these questions, I want to point out and invite reflection, first to ask ourselves, if we recognize what our talents are, that is, what we "do well." One way to recognize talent is when the activity I carry out generates concrete results. Sometimes one can recognize for oneself the possession of a talent (skill that generates a differential and results), but there are times when we are not aware of what we do well, and it is other people, our environment, who manage to highlight it in their approval and with the contribution it generates in others.

I want to highlight something I learned from a colleague.

How to detect your zone of influence? That is, how to detect where you generate an impact on the environment.

I will present a graph to expand the topic:

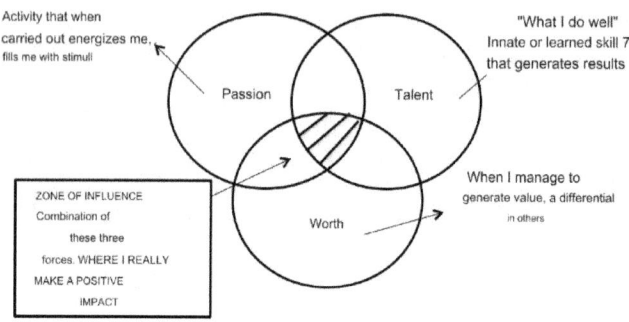

The intersection of these three aspects (passion, talent, value) mark an area where we are assertive in what we do and offer, where we have the possibility of GENERATING and GAINING. Detecting this zone of influence (which I heard from a fellow coach, Alex Berezowsky) is very important, to observe how we can move more effectively in our environments and "sell" ourselves better.

We can detect passion in activities that give us energy. Many times, there are people who find it difficult to identify what they are passionate about, what they like; the indicator of the energy returning as **feedback by doing**, generates enthusiasm and motivation. It has given me good results when it comes to accompanying these discoveries.

To talent, I would only add that many times, we can have it innately, it comes naturally to us; it is important to recognize this potential and use it intelligently. Every talent can also be developed consciously. **Talent is a skill put into assertive practice**, over and over again, until we can master it, and it becomes our ally to achieve what we want.

Courage is the ability we have to help others with our work, activity, profession, sport, etc., when we contribute and influence in a positive way; sometimes mobilizing stimuli that allow great *insights* ("realizing"), facilitating changes in those around us.

I invite you to stop and track, what are your passions, talents and your way of giving value? In this way we can analyze and determine the different areas of influence where we will generate impact.

This is the first point to start GENERATING, GAINING. A virtuous circuit is generated between what I have to GIVE and what is RECEIVED. If I have identified my area of influence, I have a very important key, then I have to know how to sell what I have to GIVE, and that circuit is a profit scheme that makes what I promote with focus materialize and return with gains ($) to my pocket, reporting desire to continue growing and generating.

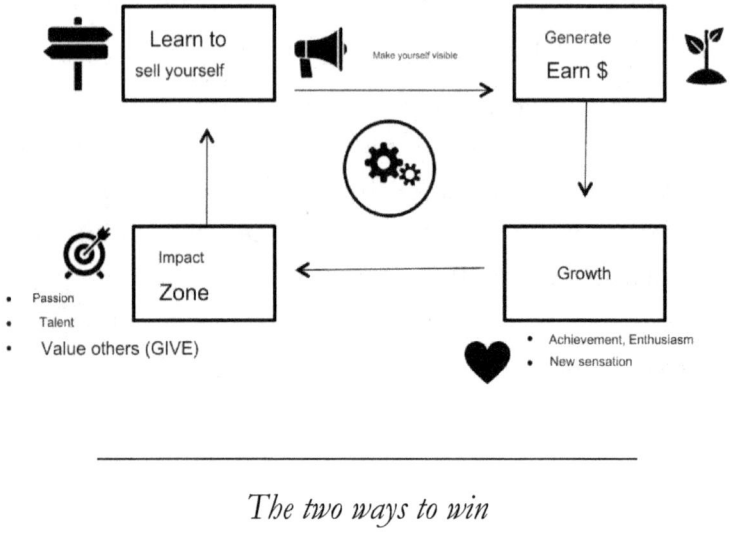

The two ways to win

In pursuit of making money, we present an aspect that is directly related to the key to administration.

As we have been sharing, emotional money management has a lot of subjective aspects that each person lives and experiences uniquely, giving money management a particularity that does not always have growth indicators. There are people who, if last month spent $50.000 in fixed costs, and this month they receive a salary increase of $20.000, perhaps at the end of this month they will begin to have a fixed cost of $70.000, as if the capital increase had not occurred. It is very common to see that even by doubling income they cannot extract profits, that is, surpluses, %

savings. When this occurs, two circumstances can occur: first, there are limiting beliefs (psycho-emotional) that prevent the person from feeling worthy of winning, of having surpluses; and on the other hand, there may be some drawbacks when it comes to managing money. We will delve into this last point shortly in this chapter.

What I want to highlight in this key (knowing how to win), is that one way to win is *managing yourself better*. For example: if my fixed costs are $20.000, but I can detect that due to poor administration there are expenses that are not necessary, and I can make adjustments to manage that flow of money more consistently and orderly, my fixed costs will surely decrease, for example, to $15.000, and through good administration, it can generate a surplus that

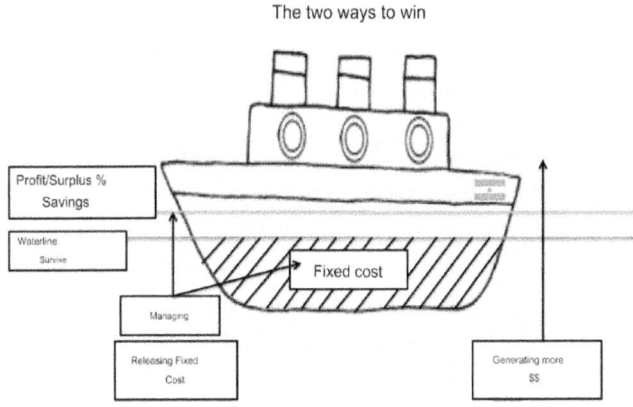

The two ways to win

automatically becomes profit; 25% is earned by good administration.

I am not wanting to stimulate restrictive administration, which is one that is based on the fear of survival and administers lack, but rather the administration that tends to order to achieve gains that will be used for the development of the person and projections of prosperity.

Managing ourselves better is a way to win and I usually advise it at the beginning of this work, because those who want to learn have no excuses to start, to carry out this aspect you only need to sit down and do it.

The other way to win, as we have been sharing, is learning to generate $. Find what you have to "give," learn to "sell it," communicate it, and make it concrete.

From this combination and balance we find two important allies, "the one who generates and the one who manages." Inseparable duo, which I always suggest when it comes to our financial life.

(Key) Know how to manage

Managing involves two specific aspects that I want to highlight and invite you to practice:

1. **Technical Aspect:** It is important to understand that financial administration has

technical and mathematical content that allow generating indicators, perspectives, projections, balances and value analysis, which are important when "managing" and making decisions. Although it is not a condition *sine qua non* having complete expertise in this aspect is a relevant point to begin to understand how to technically manage money.

To start from scratch, the most important thing will be to have a space, which can be technological (Excel, app) where we can write down the flow of our money (income-expenses). Only with clear information can we move towards good administration.

2. **Attitudinal aspect:** It is necessary to understand that whoever manages well has "control of their liquidity," by knowing where their liquid ($) goes, that is, what they spent what they generated and how and where the income impacts, generates a domain, a faucet of control and maneuver of one's own assets.

This feeling of knowing specifically that "I have available ($)," generates a feeling of mastery and poise that is essential to incorporate. We need to acquire this attitude if we want to manage abundance. If we cannot take the reins of administration, we will not be able to grow organically and with continuity towards levels of greater deployment. It is important to understand that many profits are lost due to poor management.

In the seminars that I do, there is an exercise that I invite the participants to do, which is concrete and very clear: I invite them to take a bucket and load it with water (liquidity). The water represents money, and the bucket represents administration (the containment that holds and embraces money).

In the activity, a bucket is in perfect condition (by the way, I always take new buckets0. The other bucket also appears to be in good condition, but it has holes in its surface, which cause part of the contents to fall to the ground when the water is poured into it, losing containment and consistency.

Participants take both buckets in their hands and walk 10 meters until they reach a goal; but when they arrive, they realize that one bucket has more liquidity and the other one less.

There we empirically verify that, if we do not know how to manage well, even if we are able to reach the stated objective, we arrive with less capital (liquidity) than we started with.

Many administrations are very deficient and generate in those who have them a feeling of "being lost," without direction, without clarity of what they have and what they do not have.

Liquidity and Administration

The topic of administration is so relevant that it is the first aspect we work on when we face some exercises in our seminars. Good stewardship results in standing on solid ground, and that anchoring allows a springboard for all that comes in terms of wealth; since abundance must also be managed, and the fruits and harvests of our projections will depend on said management.

In subsequent chapters we will specifically address abundance **management**, which has distinctive perspectives that will allow us to understand how surpluses, our profits, are managed.

Courage exercise to start TODAY

To manage it is not necessary to have more money, be out of debt and/or have a lot of money; every conscious work we do in this aspect will be a benefactor of growth. Any progress at this point will allow us to "plug holes in our bucket," and therefore contain the liquidity that I am losing and prepare the containment content for what I am going to generate.

The exercise that I will propose to you is simple and will allow us to understand how much money comes in and goes out over 30 days. It will require consistency and perseverance on the part of those who practice it to be able to record the flow of money day by day.

To make it very dynamic and current, you can download an expense management appl to your mobile phone (later I will share some of the most used ones) (*), where from the first day of the month we will begin to take note of each expense and each income. ; these applications allow you to add specific descriptors so that the information is organized by activity. Taking into account that the mobile phone is usually a technology that we usually have very close at hand, we will take advantage of it to instantly write down what enters and leaves my wallet.

(*) Note: Learning to use Microsoft Excel is recommended. A friend of mine said that to become CEO of a company you need to master this tool. It should be noted that if one learns dynamic tables (how to make calculations and reports) it would already be the expert level; but if you learn to manage with macros, then you can even teach others to manage.

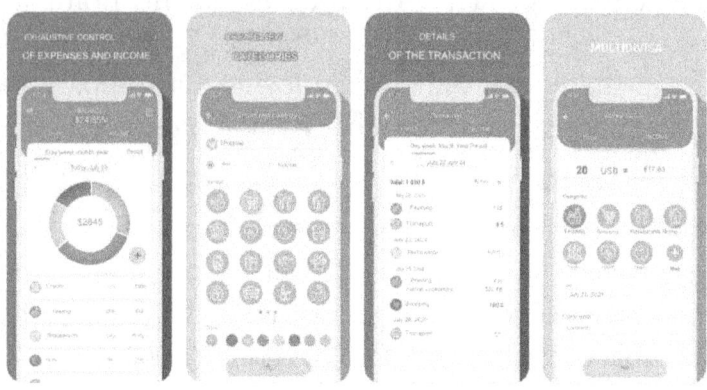

The purpose of the exercise is to know and understand the flow of money over 30 days. This will generate a concrete principle of order, which will surely make us feel better about our financial reality. Although it is an easy exercise, 50% of people fail to finish it. Facing these simple exercises highlights the weight that the issue of money has on people, on a practical level and on a subjective (psycho-emotional) level.

However, although it may seem simple, certain vices and traps that we make when purchasing in installments, using credit cards, begin to appear here. When we have debt or investment in payment in credit card installments, what do we write down in our app that month? These types of questions are very common, once these types of concerns have been overcome, we can go to the circuit of our money flow during said month, being able to objectively detect what we spend the money on and where and how my income comes from. This reality will allow us to make significant improvements, strategies and decision-making when it comes to managing ourselves better.

Let's start training the management muscle, knowing that we will need it throughout the entire journey of the money journey.

Managing ourselves does not depend on anything external to us, only on the desire to connect with our financial reality. Many avoidances of this type of follow-up are because doing so reveals our deviations and our emotional compensations put at the service of money management.

Dare to start with this step, there are many more that we will continue to learn.

(Key) Know how to save

Saving has three meanings in the dictionary that I would like to highlight:

1. tr. **Set aside a portion of your regular income.**
2. tr. **Save money as a provision for future needs.**
3. tr. **Avoid higher spending or consumption.**

Reserve, save and avoid seem to be the most prominent verbs in its definition.

I call it the triangle of good security:

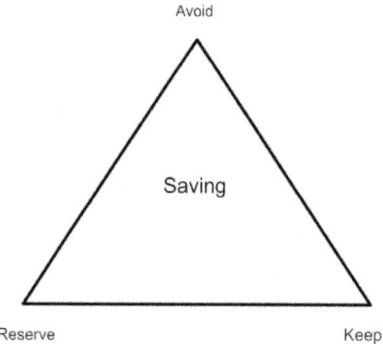

Reserving part of your ordinary income is an action that needs to be incorporated. As we shared in the chapter on "your only profit is your surplus," the first principle of profit is savings. Having reserves, having resources that can support daily living and the contingencies that arise, is an indicator of abundance.

If in our perception we do not start thinking about saving, it will never be a reality. The principle of saving begins with a decision to want to have freedom, to feel deserving, to have support and profit.

Saving money as a pension for future needs, it prepares us with more security to face situations that, if we do not have resources, could awaken in us thoughts and emotions of survival that unfocus and despair anyone. Let's think beyond money; when money approaches survival resources, it becomes vital for life, since if we cannot buy food, life indicators take on connotations of broad relevance. This is why money is sometimes perceived as something so important. Hence, many cultures that have migrated for major reasons from their country of origin, due to wars and extreme problems, have made saving a reason for living. There the reserve was sought out of fear of lack, the first savings were food to live on, then money, and in times of deployment, goods.

Avoiding higher spending or consumption allows the act of saving to incorporate a reason for good sense when spending money. If it is really considered important to achieve savings, it is necessary to moderate the "taps" of our expenses, since as we saw in the administration chapter, a lot of liquidity is lost due to emotional compensations and/or due to poor management of our assets. Avoiding an expense with a reasonable criterion is something we need to learn. This attitude always has to pursue a growth of abundance, since saving based on lack becomes very hostile and restrictive, since it is based on fear.

This is how the concept of savings traveled culturally as a principle of security that allows calming "the waters of hunger" and having the security that in any circumstance, there are resources to be able to face contingencies, and although not all situations can be resolved with those savings, the mere fact of having them predisposes the person to face situations with more poise.

---

*How do we take savings away from a lacking perspective?
How do we learn to save?*

As I said before, it does not depend on having a lot of money, it depends initially on wanting and feeling deserving of something more.

True savings has a principle of abundance and that is the intention we need in the first instance.

When children play to save, they find it fun and entertaining to accumulate capital, which they then enjoy for what really interests them.

"They save for enjoyment"

The simple and safe exercise that we can do to begin to understand and experience the concept of savings is **saving a small amount of money for 3 months**, which we will use for this exercise.

The motto is to not touch it, not use it, to pretend that it does not exist, just to keep it. I advise setting a date and time for this task, achieving a kind of ritual, where I take that portion of money and "convert" it into savings.

Setting dates to remember valuable actions is important for our brain and our perception, since we establish that this action is beginning to be necessary. Beginning to accustom our neural pathways, so that what we are practicing begins to become a necessity, is very important. The clear example of what I'm saying are the dogs of Ivan Pavlov (Russian physiologist, Nobel Prize winner in medicine in recognition of his work in the physiology of digestion, and famous for having formulated classical conditioning), who verified through a behavioral experiment, which is able to generate a hormonal segregation action associated with a pattern and a behavior.

I insist, to do this exercise it is not necessary to have a lot of money, it can even be done with coins, like children do; the act is only necessary to begin to generate a new dimension within us, "the dimension of savings."

After those three months, when we find ourselves with that money, I open to the reflection that if I could achieve it, I can continue it. And the emotion of wanting to spend or invest that money on something we like, like children, also emerges.

Here we fall into our disease of "the middle class" that saves to indulge, and although it is very good to spend money on whatever we like, we must be careful not to enter into savings and constant spending mechanisms, because in the long run it will be difficult for our savings capital to grow progressively, and with that mentality, we always tend to end up with zero in our piggy bank.

If we could for three months, **I propose to go for three more months**, when you achieve this new point by accumulating reserves for six months, we will begin to feel that it stops being a game and begins to be a reality, we would be beginning to develop a capacity that we did not have before.

However, **the next step will be that during the next month, try to save a greater amount of money**. Even at this stage it would be good to combine it with extracting that differential from money, from some better management of our daily life, from some effort, resignation, and/or additional profit that can be generated to achieve this differential; having this final goal, saving a greater amount of money, will be worth it to exercise a muscle that is beginning to gain more and more strength and consistency in us. This is the principle of abundance that I have been discussing, and why is it a principle? Because on this basis begins the opportunity to begin managing abundance, which we will see specifically in the chapter on "managing abundance."

Once I have a considerable sum, as a result of the exercise of saving, something interesting happens inside us; for the first time I have a small feeling of slack from having a reserve that is the product of a conscious learning effort. Then, from there, very diverse options open up to do with the profit capital.

Methodological Steps:

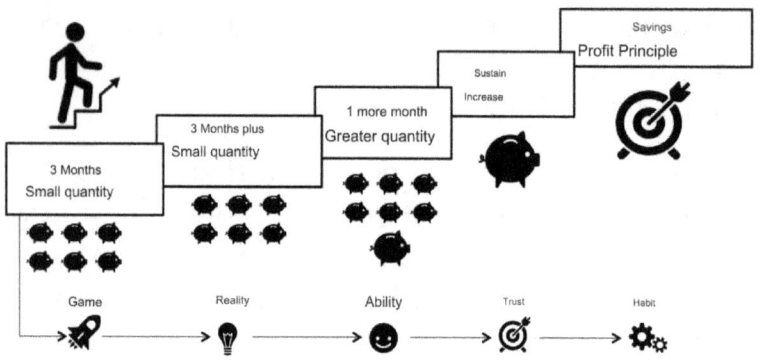

(Key) Know how to Invest

Here we come to a much more relevant key, could we say the key to abundance?

This is how it looks in the panorama of wealth, the truth is that when we make good investments, we get richer. People who manage this key have the experience of seeing how their initial capital increases considerably. If we understand money as energy, the sensation that is felt when the energy is doubled, when it is magnified, is remarkable. It is perhaps for this reason that many people lose their way when they suddenly increase their money, they do not know how to codify the management of its volume.

The truth is that investment, far from being a game of luck, is a field of a lot of analysis, strategy and knowledge.

The first point to understand is that when one invests, it is done with capital, which is the product of one's own or someone else's profit.

Profit capital has a history, a force, a weight in itself; that is why it has value and can be used to positively influence another good and receive more value for contributing to said investment.

Profit, as the chapter on managing abundance describes, has four paths to follow (Saving, Enjoyment, Giving, Investment).

- **Saving** is a reserve of value that allows us the psychological and factual security of being able to cope with contingencies.

- **Enjoyment** allows the ability to have the means to have quality of life.

- **The act of "giving"** opens the door for us to help others, to return the good received and satisfy our transcendent concerns.

- **Investment** has the exclusive purpose of increasing the initial capital; where the first investment, to be a good investor, is to invest in learning.

What is investing then?

We could define it as "Using an amount of money, capital, in a project or business to achieve profits."

It is a mechanism that increases, enlarges, that betters what enters it. The investment triangle will be the following:

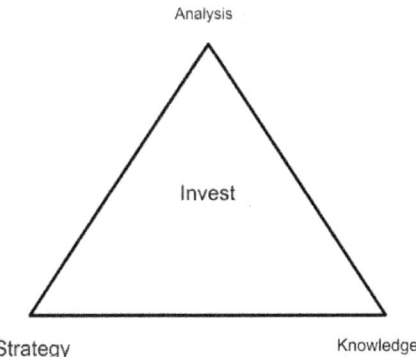

These three concepts are very important to begin to understand the mind of a good investor; both a more innate assertive investor and someone more studious in the matter have these three dimensions when investing their capital.

He who invests well always tends to make a good **analysis** of the context and the investment goal; the analysis of the potential investment product is decisive to begin to focus with more interest on its goal.

When investing, for example, in a capital market instrument, the investor analyzes, in the case of shares, that the company of origin has solid fundamentals; it also analyzes the history of the different movements of the stock curves (technical analysis), verifies the sociopolitical and macroeconomic context, to see how it can influence the stock market, and thus influence the investment goal, etc.

If it were another type of investment, for example, the purchase of a house, the same criterion also influences, the good investor must analyze the area where it is located, its quality, its potential with possible improvements, the level of turnover of the area in the case of selling it, etc. In both cases, the type of risk that one wants to take is specifically analyzed. The risk indicator is a determining element for investing and for defining the investor's profile.

There is a high-risk profile; by taking more risk, you can obtain more profit in the type of product you invest in. The moderate profile maintains a conservative base, but usually leaves a percentage of its capital (smaller) to use in higher risk investments. And the conservative profile invests in more stable instruments, which emit a low-yield profit, but which can be regulated over time and with good security backing.

Another element of the investor triangle is **strategy.** When investing, develop a strategy taking into account the "why" of the investment. In my experience I have proven that investing without clear goals disorganizes the tactical movements that are made, bad decisions are made and the focus of what is important is lost. For example, if the "why" of my investment is to obtain $200.000 to buy a house, and I invest in a stock that manages to give me that profit at a point in its upward curve; that moment is the indicated time to **withdraw profit** and get hold of said capital. It has happened to me, and I have also seen in others, that by expecting more profit in the upward trend, the capital is not withdrawn at the indicated time, and after a while the action collapses, losing the opportunity that surpassed the initial goal.

The "why" is decisive. Studying accessory aspects, such as tax issues, interests, lawyer costs, procedures, professionals, commissions and other aspects, are of great importance in putting together the strategy to be implemented.

And the great ally for assertiveness is **knowledge**, the more we understand about the area in which we are investing, the greater the point of assertiveness will be. It is very important, in terms of finances, to be able to and know how to ask for help from professionals who have full knowledge of what they do. Although it is important that we consciously learn everything we can, a lot of time is saved when we invest in good professionals who advise with their knowledge.

With the investment pyramid we can understand in depth how an investor observes life.

How can I start investing?

Like all learning, it is important to start small and well advised.

If you were to invest in any stock in the stock market; I would try not to get carried away by friends' tendencies and trivial information, unless we know someone who is very knowledgeable on the subject, I would look for a knowledgeable person to ask for this type of advice. Let us keep in mind that when we invest, we are putting into play capital already achieved, perhaps the product of a lot of effort, and it is important to put ourselves in the hands of competent people to protect or minimize the risk and also understand the projection of said investment.

The first point is then to get advice, start investing with small sums of money, **have the experience of profit**. This point is important because it breaks the belief and stereotype of winning with effort. Let's think that when we invest in stocks, for example, we get on a moving train (the company), and we get money without any effort. This paradigm shift generates a before and an after in the life of any investor.

Another relevant point, as we said in previous paragraphs, **is withdrawing from the investment on time**. A good investor achieves the goal and exits the game. It is always a good indicator to withdraw profits, **having a wallet with bills always generates belonging and trust**.

For financial education, consciously reaching the investor's key is almost "the goal," the last subject to be performed; given that **knowing how to invest** contemplates in a certain way the knowledge of knowing how to earn, knowing how to save and knowing how to manage.

In its psycho-emotional aspect, investing is associated with the value and care given to the initial good. How much is the fruit of one's own effort that will be put into action at the time of investing valued? The most notable point is that if we learn to invest, we begin to specifically earn money, in this sense we begin to live more comfortably, and not all of us are willing to take the risk of that change.

That is why, if done consciously, the risk and vertigo generated by this type of reality can be realized gradually and fully.

Cheer up

It is important to get to the key to the investor, it allows us to have experiences that build the confidence of those who practice it.

What I usually observe is that the person that loses their fear of the concept of investing, begins to understand more deeply what it entails, and ends up realizing that it is much easier to invest conscientiously, than perhaps to do more conventional jobs, with a "safe" hat on, but that imply an amount of mental and physical energy that can be used on **analysis, strategy and knowledge.**

Cheer up, it's a long road, but when you start, it opens up a new world in the way we think about money and our finances.

The four triangles

Rescuing the main elements of the four keys, they derive 4 triangles with central concepts to take into account and develop in practice.

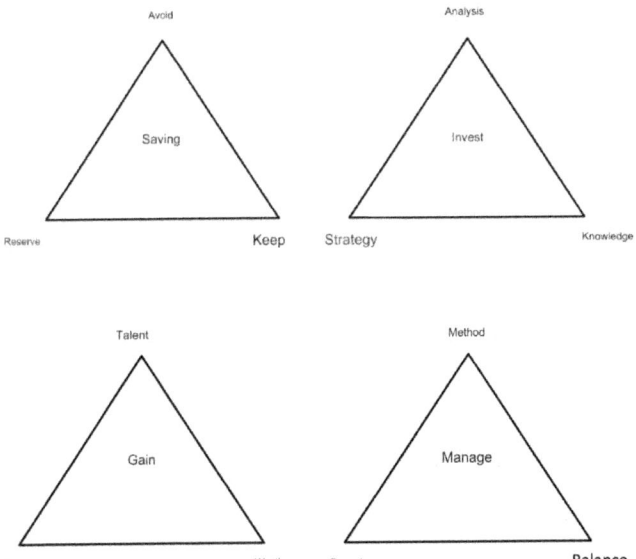

Managing these 12 concepts ensures consistent financial health. In the methodological part we will generate integrations of these value points that show a clear map to be carried out in the use of these 4 master keys.

Your profit is always your surplus

$

Revenue

A person, today a very close friend, who at the time I received at a consultation for a specific topic, gave me the key to what I am going to tell you about below. Not only did he provide me with a key that changed my **perspective**, but also, it made me experience in reality what he wanted to explain to me in response to a question that I, with all sincerity, asked him one afternoon in my office.

Knowing his life and his story, with which we worked on his personal development, I had observed that his financial activity had grown a lot.

His consultation process was already concluding, we were in the closing and balance meetings, I still remember that afternoon, cold autumn in Argentina.

"I feel so good!" he expressed happily when greeting me.

Serenity and gratitude could be seen in him. We began a more relaxed conversation, and although it was not the focus of the topic, I decided to ask him something that worried me, that came to me almost spontaneously.

"I would like to ask you: **How do you "think" about money?"**

Perhaps, now that I reflect on it, I felt identified with his life, and there was a reflection of projection that motivated me to ask him such a question.

"Do you want me to teach you?" he responded, looking at me and smiling. It was as if he already knew that one day I would ask him that question.

"Yes of course."

I was taken aback by his response, but I quickly retorted. There was a very particular complicity in the atmosphere, it seemed for a moment that the roles were changing.

"**Let's start now.** Are you up for it?"

"Come on."

I took a breath, settled into my seat, I felt like a spectator about to start a movie. I clearly sensed that I was going to leave my comfort zone.

"What you are going to understand with all this is that... YOUR PROFIT IS ALWAYS YOUR SURPLUS, if you don't understand this point, you will never win. Let me explain..."

«My *profit is my "surplus"*» I began to reflect.

"For this practical training, you will only have to invest four dollars."

"And what are these four dollars for?"

"Calm down, let's go in parts. To learn we have to calm down. I noticed that you recently bought a car that is impeccable. Do you want to sell it?"

"No, I just bought it."

"Point approved, **not wanting to sell, or not being in a hurry to sell the good on which I want to make a good profit.** Now I'm going to tell you what to do with those four dollars."

Then he calmly began to explain four steps I should follow:

The first step was to take good photos of the car with my phone, as if I was going to sell it. Photos of something to sell should always have **proper context** that inspires quality, good care. «*Marketing and visual impact is the first step in sales*».

The second and third step was always to be exact, and clearly understand where to sell, which is why I had to spent those four dollars on advertising the car on an internet site (free market) with a prominent place to have dissemination.

The fourth and most important step was to publish it **25% more expensive than the average market value**.

"And who is going to buy it from me at 25% more?" I asked in amazement. He smiled with some irony.

"Wasn't it that you didn't want to sell it? Do what I tell you, surrender to the experience to learn."

That afternoon I complied up to phase three. I did everything he told me step by step, and three days later I had the car I had just bought listed for sale. Crazy!

I was wondering if I was going to get any questions. After a few days, interested parties began to arrive, some wanted to exchange my car for another, others wanted to take it as part payment for a piece of land or a house, others asked me what the difference was that justified its price, etc. Anyway, my idea that there would be no consultations was a *limiting belief*, those interested were willing to ask; I began to reflect that **a good price always attracts.**

I called this friend to share that they were asking me questions about the sale.

"I told you, don't worry, we're doing well."

"What do I do now?"

"Nothing; or rather, keep listening to proposals, **your power today is that you do NOT want to sell the car**" he answered me, smiling with his explanation.

Two weeks passed and a call came on my cell phone. I don't usually answer calls from strangers, but that day I answered. It was a lady interested in my car. After the greeting, she tells me:

"If the car is in the condition described in the advertisement, I will buy it at the published price; I prefer to pay more and purchase a good item" she tells me concretely and with authority, "If it's okay with you, I'd like to go see it today."

"Madam, thank you for your offer, let me to call you in 10 minutes" I didn't know what to say.

I quickly called "my business mentor" at that point and told him the situation.

"Good. Now let's go for more... with the offer in hand I ask you again: do you want to sell it?" the question threw me off again. "If you sell it for twenty five thousand dollars, you can then buy the same car for twenty, which is the market value, you will make a profit of five thousand dollars! How does that sound?"

"You're out of your mind!" At that moment I felt an energy that encouraged me to move forward.

I made an appointment with the lady; she came with the deposit and after four days the car was sold and transferred.

And now that?

At the next meeting with my "commercial mentor" he congratulated me by telling me that the first phase had been approved. For my part, I had already investigated the possibility of purchasing the same car model and I was happy with what I had experienced. I had earned five thousand dollars as a result of what I had learned.

"Are we going for more?" he stared at me again with his defiant tone of voice.

"Come on" I responded, intrigued by the situation.

I had incorporated an important skill; **saying yes, many times, opens many doors.**

"What car would you like to buy?" he asked me seriously.

"The same one, as we had agreed."

"**Think big,** what car do you want now?"

There was a pause, a silence. With doubts but curiosity, I shared with him that I would like a Toyota model that I had been looking at, but that was not worth the money it had at the market value.

"I knew you were going for more. Who told you that we are going to buy it at the basic market value?"

"What!?" I was beginning to reflect if this mentor friend had lost his sanity. «He's crazy.»

Inspiring me with great confidence, he began to explain to me that I should enter the same internet website and look for the Toyota model that I wanted to buy and that I should offer all candidates 20% less than what they are asking for.

Market

You have to understand that in the market there are always buyers who for some reason need a quick sale, and that quick sale offers a solution to a problem that they need to solve; offers allow them access to their solution. **This has to be the mindset and perspective so that our attitude is always the winner**, understanding all the rules of the game of this market and any market.

I did what he told me, and within 15 days I had bought the Toyota that I longed for, with the peculiarity that I had acquired it 20% below the average market value.

Learning

I learned to **negotiate higher values** (to defend the good that one has), to not rush, to have the firmness to wait for the right offer, the one I am looking for.

I also learned to **negotiate lower values**, being able to understand how markets for the exchange of goods truly move; how the comprehensive needs of buyers and sellers generate endless opportunities when it comes to wanting to achieve what one wants to achieve.

Understanding the rules of the game removed many limiting beliefs from me, which did not allow me to defend and price my assets at a high value, nor to understand and be able to negotiate, persuade and capitalize on opportunities offered by the exchange market.

But what I take away, as most important in this experience, is letting myself be carried away by the impulse to sincerely ask this friend what I needed, **that "bath of humility" opened the door to everything else**.

Perhaps many people are willing to teach us and help us, we are the ones who need to put ourselves in the position of apprentice to receive the abundance that is waiting for us.

Nowadays, every time I meet my friend, we share how important that experience was for me, in terms of my financial education; and he often shares that it was the least he could do, after the help he had received in his personal development process.

Balance manifests itself again here as an indicator of abundance, where when one receives, one tends to generously correspond with the good received.

And so, the wheel continues, sharing with you this experience that opened my eyes on that occasion, and that filled my desire to continue growing with attitude and enthusiasm.

If time is not enough, you are in lack

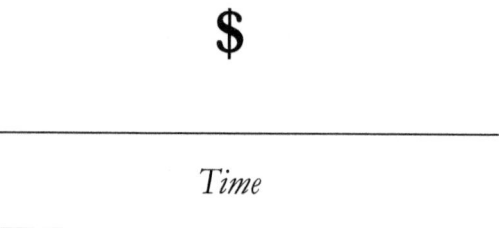

Time

Our lifespan cannot be recovered. Therefore, those who do not manage time well lose quality of life. It is a topic with great vertices to analyze. I invite you to review in the annexes to the book, a chapter of the book (<u>*Shelters Camino*</u>) of my authorship, where I deepen the importance of understanding linear time and subjective time.

Returning to time in relation to money and abundance, I want to emphasize that I understand it as **an indicator** from where we can measure ourselves and reflect on whether we are "restricting time or expanding time."

Restricted time

When time on a linear or subjective level feels very restricted, we have the feeling that it is not enough; on many occasions, "time runs on us," "it drowns us," "it governs us." I sense that you understand what I'm telling you, 80% of the world's population lives with these sensations. From this perception of time, the quality of life is lacking; even people with a lot of money are the ones who suffer the most from this "time disease." Something from the root is wrong here, in how the conquest of the feeling of freedom and happiness is channeled. Many times, we think that if we had money everything would be different, although many perspectives change, the patterns that make us "free or slaves" live in our psycho-emotional and perceptual reality, it is not in vain that we dedicate the first part of this book to delve deeper into the meaning we give money.

The emotional compensations that we make in pursuit of a chimerical freedom, "if we had more money," mean that our time is restricted to this pretension, which only delays, precisely in time, the possibility of truly learning how to achieve a wide and abundant life.

I know very capable and intelligent people, who never have time for anything, not even to answer a phone call or message. Take this point as an indicator of abundance or lack.

He who, being active, has time, is a person who surely has a long life (pillars of abundance).

Extending time

When time expands, its domain appears, the person seems to decide what to do, chooses by understanding and distinguishing what is important from what is superfluous (prioritizes). Nobody stops us, because we are the drivers, based on our decisions.

Here emotional plenitude appears, when a person attends to the important needs that govern their life, adjusts time to those priorities and acts accordingly, generating congruence between what they want and do, and always decides based on them. Achieving this scheme allows us to be the protagonist and responsible for our time.

This person lives abundantly, time is associated with their values, what they consider important to live, on this conveyor belt of experiences, which is time.

Practice

From 0 to 10, how do you spend your time?

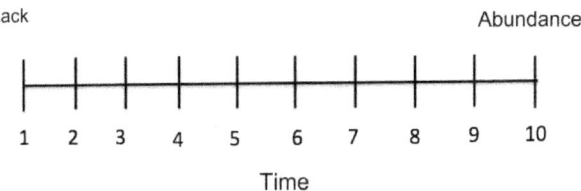

Reflect on it:

Do you master time?

Does time drown you?

Write your answers in your log.

Reflection

Try to redesign your time management, based on "what is important," the true reasons that move your life. You can guide yourself with the 4 pillars of abundance to rethink different aspects where there may be time dedicated and chosen. Write yourself a map of activities that take time, but that represent important bases for you.

Record how you feel when your life becomes coherent. This record generates fullness and "air to climb another step."

Time management is one of the pillars of money management. I would like to share specific habits that will help you in everyday life:

Use your time well, don't waste it with worthless activities.

Don't get caught up in constant device interruptions. You are in control of them, not the other way around. Be attentive, respond to all messages. I have learned that generally people with abundance answer all the messages that interest them and that they receive. Not receiving a response means there is no interest. On the other hand, people who are in lack respond late. How would you feel if you went to a restaurant, and they brought your food 3 hours late? Why do you get angry with this delay? And when a colleague, friend or family member messages you and you take days to respond?

It is important that you be direct with time, do not turn it around, do not try to deceive it with tricks. It makes no sense to set your alarm clock for a specific time and then get into the habit of "sleeping" for half an hour more. The body doesn't work like that, you have simply interrupted a good sleep, to have a bad dream for half an hour. Take care of your body and watch your watch, be punctual, don't waste time. Take advantage of the morning, sleep your 8 or 9 hours a day fully with a true rest.

Being punctual with yourself and with others is the basis of a spirit of abundance.

Here I stop and want to share with you that abundance is about being generous with your time and lack is about being miserly with it. Think about it. You can tell me that you have a hard time managing money, but time? Everyone has the same number of minutes each day, 1,440 minutes. Be a protagonist, not a victim of time.

Managing abundance

$

Manage your future

As we have been learning, administration is key to our kit in our 4 keys to a rich man.

One way to manage is to manage sensibly, minimizing emotional compensations, our fixed costs. This administration, as we shared in previous chapters, gives us security and confidence when it comes to knowing where our income and expenses truly go. Mastering this "tap" control usually generates emotional stability and "the desire to go for more." When we organize ourselves in this sense, we feel a stimulus to face new learnings.

The other way of managing, which I want to present to you below, is the one that will allow us to manage our surpluses, that is, our profits.

Below I present a practical resource that will allow you to organize and simplify the practice of how to manage abundance.

The 4 Little Pigs (Piggy Banks)

This will be our excuse to incorporate a concept that can truly change our way of **managing our quality of life**.

Surely some of can remember the time in our childhood when it was common to receive a piggy bank as a gift, to stimulate the habit of saving from a young age. I remember they used to be made of porcelain. When it was decided to use said savings for some goal, it had to be broken; I still hear the noise against the floor and the feeling of happiness when accessing the handful of coins and some bills, which allowed us to buy what we dreamed of.

The concept of savings is strongly installed in the culture, as we mentioned in previous chapters, it contains concepts associated with effort, discipline, perseverance; and the established tradition phrase, that "savings are not to be used," except in emergency situations.

Although at first, I was not convinced on this idea, that savings should not be touched, today with the criterion of "the 4 little pigs," I share and agree with this statement, which we will briefly explain.

Let us remember that abundance, according to our analysis and experience, is based on 4 pillars.

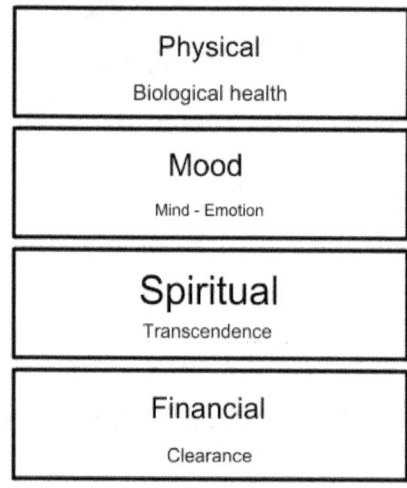

When managing abundance, these pillars should be represented, and that is what the resource we are getting to is about.

Here, we introduce 4 fundamental concepts from which we are going to manage our profit, always with a *clear direction* of generating abundance, seeking the necessary balance to prioritize needs and expectations.

Savings (Piggy Bank)

Saving is a good that "allows us to sleep peacefully." The purpose of savings is to have reserves, which enable us to face difficulties and unforeseen events that may arise.

Human beings have an instinct for self-preservation, which also influences our mental life and that we must always take into account; to this instinct, which is like a hungry lion, we need to keep it well fed, since if basic needs are threatened in a real or imaginary way, thoughts of worry and fear could arise that make it difficult to grow and plan for the future.

This also happens at a biological level, we have an area of the brain called the hypothalamus, which precisely works on this instinct of self-preservation in the face of danger, releasing an endless number of hormones to defend ourselves. In this state of our nervous system (sympathetic) it is very difficult to feel abundance. Therefore, the money that is in savings **"can't be touched,"** in this way the lion of instinct is always fed.

Investment (Piggy Bank)

The money in the investment piggy bank is intended for learning, with the aim of "greening our garden" and achieving profits on the invested capital. It is intended for learning because precisely to know how to invest you have to prepare, educate yourself, take risks, often win and also lose to learn.

The money in this piggy bank can be lost, and it shouldn't affect our mood that much. This money already has to be generated from this purpose of irrigation and learning.

Giving (Piggy Bank)

Giving is the need that a person has to return to others, to society, part of the good received.

Learning to Give is not easy; it is not just putting your hand in your pocket; true Giving requires empathetically understanding what that person specifically needs and being able to provide some resource that always guarantees good for that person.

The generous action of providing resources to others usually generates very pleasant sensations in those who practice it. The truth is that very wealthy people tend to donate resources to worthy causes.

Starting to manage money to donate is quite revolutionary, but it's just a matter of putting your mind to it.

Enjoyment (Piggy Bank)

The money for enjoyment is generated precisely to use it in everything that implies quality of life. Each person will decide which aspects are relevant to feeling that they are enjoying themselves (travel, clothing, properties, experiences, etc.). Allocating money to this piggy bank is central. Our spirit feels very stimulated when we enjoy it. Enjoyment at a biological level generates a state of serenity, which allows, in the right measure, moments of great unfolding and a favorable field for projecting new horizons.

Managing piggy banks

To healthily manage these piggy banks, it is important that the generated profit has the concept that this sum of money is going to be divided into four equal parts; and that each of these parts will have a specific function and purpose. It is very important that profit is generated from this conception and attitude.

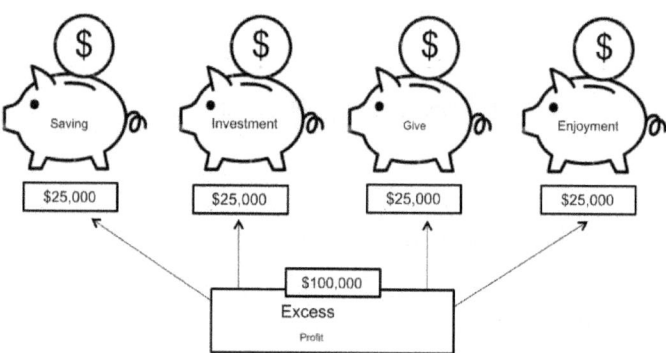

We are very used to all the profit going to the savings piggy bank; and if we are very fond of not touching our savings, we are left without money to enjoy, invest and Give (thus living with savings, we live in lack). We have already seen how these imbalances arise in the chapter on the 4 keys of a rich person (knowing how to save, manage, earn and invest). That is why "where" we do it from will be key for each liquidity ($) to take the channel of abundance for which it was created.

Looking at the graph, it is clear to see how to manage the profit in 4 equal parts, although many times the Giving piggy bank is of 10% or 15%; only in very abundant people does it reach the indicated 25%.

Let us remember then: savings "are not touched" (intended to preserve instinct). Investment, money allocated to learn how to increase my assets. Giving returns to others and society part of the good received; and enjoyment, money allocated to expand our quality of life.

Practice

I specifically advise you to start managing your surpluses in this way, it is not necessary to buy 4 piggy banks, although many times this gesture represents an anchoring ritual to achieve this type of changes. Each of these "little pigs" represents an archetypal concept to incorporate and assimilate; and it can be represented in Excel, in an App, in a notebook, on a whiteboard, where you can have a record and follow-up of the administration of this liquidity.

This exercise consolidates the importance of continuing to re-educate our perception in the true concept of profit, always reminding our brain of the new knowledge to incorporate, if we really want to continue climbing the steps.

The debt of the one who looses and the one who wins

$

Living in Debt

The first reflection to share is that debt is the product and result of credit.

Before having debt, someone always trusted us, we were given a credit of value and that is where we acquired what we understand as debt.

For South American countries, the concept of debt does not have good repercussions, since in these latitudes and cultures, in general terms, good use of this resource has not always been made; this can generate situations where the debt becomes an ordeal.

These situations occur because sometimes credit-debt is acquired without much prior analysis of what the entire process that is experienced in order to pay it off entails; but in the vast majority of cases, debt is contracted to be able to get out of pressing situations, where it is already owed, and another debt is mounted on top of that situation to get out of debt. Although it may seem like a tongue twister and somewhat illogical, there are cultures and people who live from debt to debt. In general, this system of action keeps the person experiencing it in an internal state of anxiety and lack, because that sensation of being below the waterline promotes survival to be activated, generating these sensations of emergency. From this explanation it derives that people have the meaning of "debt as something negative."

Bad Debt

This type of debt is the one we have been sharing in the previous paragraph. It is a credit resource that is obtained to be able to get out of some pressing situation, and that due to lack of foresight as to how to pay off said debt, it generates a feeling of lack and lability in those who experience it. This type of debt affects all social classes, it is observed in families with low resources, who need to request credit-debt to continue living, but it is also observed in wealthier classes, where the poor administration of their assets puts them in pressing situations, and they have to resort to debt to compensate for their poor money management. There is poor basic administration, they do not solve the problem, and they live over and over again in that mechanism.

Of course, it is also seen very objectively in the political systems of many countries, that due to their bad administrations and corruption they live in debt for the future and try to accommodate the present with short-term credit-debt, which only further complicates the panorama.

Good Debt

I like to define this debt as an opportunity.

I still remember with great gratitude, when in my youth I wanted to buy my first car, and I had been able to save 40% of its value. In my mind I made a linear projection of the time it would take me to generate the remaining 60%, and I was distressed to know that the time was long, based on the salary I had at that time; I remember how distressed I was by that feeling of wanting something, and having to wait too long to get it.

My older brother, who knew about my desire, told me with complete ease, why don't you ask for a personal loan? You can pay it with the savings margin that you have today; and in that way you obtain the good now and you commit to paying it overtime.

I still remember the happiness I felt, understanding that, by asking for credit and taking on debt, I could achieve what I wanted in a timely manner. There I experienced how debt was transformed into an opportunity, and how that mechanism allowed me to fulfill expectations of abundance that I had at that moment. This example recreates what good debt means, which opens up possibilities for us and, far from putting us in pressing situations, allows us to advance in our growth using a mechanism adapted to the economic reality of each case, where its due compliance allows us to achieve what we long for.

It is important to understand that to acquire good debt, we must carry out a conscious analysis of how we are going to face the portions of debt that will be paid overtime, and also analyze how solvent we are, in financial terms, so that credit institutions, and/or people give us a loan, that is, they trust us.

This analysis and balance will depend in some way on whether what we are acquiring is good debt or bad debt.

He who wins and he who loses

The one who wins, that is, the one who generates surpluses of value, will always use debt as an element of a larger strategy.

Part of emotional and financial stability is to be able to build a strategy where **good debt is a bridge that allows you to fulfill the space** that you are planning with enthusiasm.

The debt of the loser usually starts from a foundation of lack, where the ground, the emotional and financial pillars are very unstable; from this perspective it is logical to think that credit-debt requests will follow a more complicated path, one of chaos and little consistency.

Everything is based on debt

This statement happens after several reflections associated with the world of money and also in existential terms.

For example: many technical investments instruments work under the pattern of debt, using it as a bridge of credit and trust that is deposited in certain assets. On a personal existential level, something similar also happens with the opportunity to live. I still remember a phrase my parents told me: "We collaborate to give your life, now you have a debt with creation to dignify it."

It is important that we can understand the concept of debt with content and knowledge, since it is a very important mean and resource to grow, expand and achieve abundance.

You write the future

$

The future is not yet written

Days ago, I wrote the following sentence in an article:

"Don't look so far back, take the risk of finding what's coming."

Although I liked the phrase that I was able to reflect on and express, I still see it as a bit restricted, since by wanting to find what is coming, I am assuming that there is a certain destination.

I go for more; based on what we share and some other premises that science brings in relation to the atom, which some quantum scientists eloquently develop, the human being has a world of possibilities at his feet, which he can choose consciously and voluntarily. This proven reality means that each of us writes our destiny.

I want to remove from my reflection all magical thoughts that make us think that just by setting out to do something, we will achieve it. I invite the good sense to know that we have to prepare for some displacements to occur, but it is true that when a heartfelt and overcoming purpose is combined with a mental projection consistent with that goal, and our will is set in motion by also executing some movements of "doing," it seems as if something "magical" occurred presenting a map of synchronicity that seems to materialize the dream, or the purpose that gave rise to the entire movement.

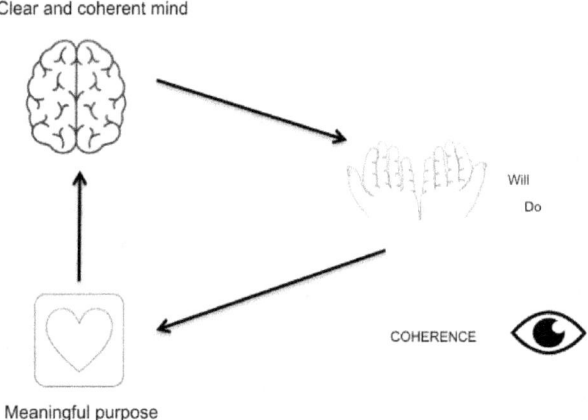

At this point it doesn't matter where you come from, the most important thing is where you want to go.

Let's start designing that future now. When I say **"design now"** I mean the possibility of really choosing what you want, how you want to live, with what perspectives, with what ease and fullness.

Try to design it in your mind, describe and savor all kinds of details, maintain your intention and attention; when you try to do it, thoughts will come trying to distract you, take you away from your best scene, "what you are thinking has nothing to do with your reality," "nothing you are imagining is possible," voices from your past will always be speaking to you.

This type of dialogue is normal, what is tragic is when that dialogue does not exist and your conditioning from the past regulates your life.

Open the possibility to create your life.

The image you put in your mental retina is very powerful, it will also have to be supported by a real and deep desire to achieve that life you dream of.

To turn a new leaf in your life you will need courage, vertigo will come to your door to show you that change is coming, if you are trying to learn, do not fear, vertigo is nothing more than an indicator that you have entered new areas.

Embrace the possibility that what you dream of already exists in you, it is just a new step to find it.

Synthesis 3

Part 3: LEARN

- Financial education. Understand the "why" of training
- 4 Ways to live with money
- The 4 keys that contain the domain of $
- Story of value, Dare to ask
- The importance of your time
- Manage your abundance (piggy banks)
- The growth debt
- Be brave, Design and conquer your future

This PART 3 of the book is about learning, acquiring knowledge through study or experience. Here I want to stop; money management requires practical knowledge, not just academic knowledge.

When you lose money in a business, many times you don't lose it, it has been invested in experience, and the balance of whether it was worth it (the experience) is what we determine as the value of the money. If it had value, it was worth it. So? Always dedicate yourself to DO actions that you like and that are valuable. When you don't like something or it doesn't have value, that's when you're wasting money.

The first step in this section is financial education, it is important to understand the principle of an interest rate (if you want to know more about the comparison of real rates adjusted for inflation I recommend reading FISHER), but at the beginning it is important that you know what savings, budget, debt, rates, dividends, investment, diversification, assets, liabilities, income, risks, rewards, indices, returns and other concepts that I have shared with you mean.

I like to quote Robert Kiyosaki, it is important to understand the flow of money, when it comes in and when it goes out. Buying a house for $400.000 has different annual maintenance than offices for the same economic value. It is important to understand that we generate money on a recurring basis with our body (employed or self-employed) or when we have other ways to get to it (owner, investor).

In the same way that we take care of our body, among other things by measuring our fever, our investments also have a thermometer, but an emotional one.

Knowing how to earn, knowing how to save, knowing how to manage and knowing how to invest become business keys, emotional keys, keys that open doors.

Above all, we need courage, defined as the impetuous decision and effort of the spirit, our bravery. In this book we talk about encouragement and the lack of it. I would like to share with you as a summary that having courage is taking care of our spirit and the bases for this are knowing how to learn, and always staying active.

PART 4

Practice! Develop habits!

The idea is to be practical, not to philosophize or make major academic repairs, since there is a saying that says that the philosopher is the one who gives advice to others about difficulties that he has not experienced.

Practical experience *is one of the bases of wisdom.*

Methodology to change

$

Shift mechanism

The methodology presents, based on this book, the opportunity to generate concrete changes regarding financial education.

To do this, the method consists of 4 fundamental pillars:

1. **Review:**

    Reviewing will allow, throughout the process, the possibility of maintaining conscious attention to be able to remove beliefs, promote learning and be able to move opportunities that allow us to achieve patterns of abundance.

2. **Take action:**

    Proactivity will be an indicator and a primary attitude to have the energy to venture to experience changes. In action many prejudices are demolished and one's strength is tested.

3. **Learn:**

The specific need to incorporate knowledge that allows us to understand and comprehend new possibilities and tools. Without a learning process (3 brains) it is impossible to change.

4. **Practice and develop habits:**

Practice. Training will be the most entertaining and the most concrete. What will really define our progress and our gaps to cover. Habits will be what determine our achievement, our new identity, our sustainable change.

Methodological approach

Method

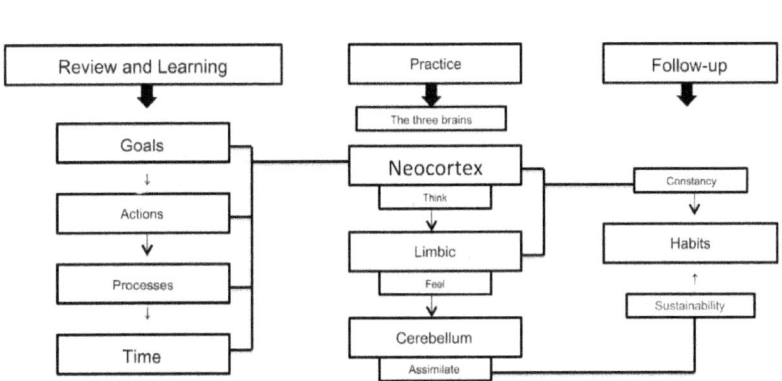

The method approach allows a stage of **"review and learning,"** where new knowledge, new perspectives, new meanings are unlearned and learned.

In order for this new knowledge to enter our perceptual framework and really be a real change in your life, they need **"obligatory of practice,"** which will allow, under the described process, to assimilate new possibilities and development.

Consistency in these indicators of change will generate in our reality what we have been looking for since we began this book, new habits in your relationship with money. These will be the concrete indicators of change, from which we can evaluate our transformations, thus achieving the initial purpose.

The method consists of 4 fundamental pillars (review, act, learn, practice) that will be articulated and intertwined in the training, thus being able to achieve comprehensive movements to achieve transversal dynamism in learning.

Let's start!

Training manual

We will use a training manual, a travel log that will allow us to face the first 3 months of practice. In this book we will provide training criteria, so that you can do it with an attitude of "personal self-management"; that allows you to record step by step many of the contents provided and put them into practice.

Although we will develop the common thread of the training in this book, you can contact me through LinkedIn and social networks to request the instructions and files to register the travel log and so that you have the training material organized and with enough spaces to complete with your personal information. Request *"your own learning log."*

The entire comprehensive cycle of financial education can take us 9 months of practice (a good start), but in this book we will present a three month training, which will allow concrete changes. Based on this shift of change, confidence in oneself is consolidated and we will be able to carry out more complex learning in the future.

Month 1

Preparation

- Initial suggestion: If we start the training on the 1st day of the month, it will allow us a clearer order in some follow-up aspects, although it is not a determining condition.

- Context: The first week of work we need to prepare some elements that will be necessary for our action and practice; just as an athlete prepares his clothing for training. If we do it, there will be a greater willingness and desire to start.

- Each week of training will have 7 key points to do.

Items needed to get started:

1- **Four piggy banks / Rite and creativity**: make and build with the materials you like (cardboard, plastic, ceramics, etc.), the 4 piggy banks of abundance. Although "we are digital," if we manifest some symbol with our hands, it is a more concrete way of appropriating more strongly a tool that we will use.

2- **Expense manager download**: Download an expense manager application to your cell phone and/or create a spreadsheet in Microsoft Excel or Google Sheets where you can enter your income and expenses in the future, dividing them by activity. I initially recommend the cell phone app for this training since it will be an element that we will always have on hand to load the information instantly and thus achieve more agility.

3- **Training log**: You need to have a specific notebook to write down the activities and resonances that occur during the program. As we said, below I leave you a guide to sheets designed in an orderly way so that you can print them.

These 3 elements will accompany us during the three months trip.

Week 1

1- Starting on day 1, start entering your day-to-day income and expenses into your expense manager. Here we will begin to train consistency in being aware of how the flow of your money moves, "just write it down," keep a cool mind, write it down and that's it.

2- Reread the Introduction from this book *(page 13)* and ask yourself:

   What does money mean in your life?

   - Write down what comes to your mind and your feelings:

Thoughts	Feel/Sensations

3- Motivation to change (you can reread the section "<u>Motivation to change</u>," page , in part 1 of this book).

<u>It is important to ask yourself valuable questions:</u>

What is your relationship with money today?

_____

_____

Has money been an ally or a limitation in your life?

_____

_____

What country were you born in? Do you reside in the country of birth?

_____

_____

How is the economy in the country you live in? Is stable? Is it of growth? Is it unstable?

_____

What motivates you to change in relation to money?

Why do you want to improve that relation?

_____

_____

4- Review how you act with money today.

Reread the section "<u>Let's review your doing</u>," page , of Part

Ask yourself basic aspects of your financial reality today:

Do you have a record of what your exact income is?

_____

_____

Do you know what the flow of your expenses is like? Where does the money you spend go?

_____

_____

Do your profits grow over time, are they static, do they have development plans?

_____

_____

Order, discipline and perseverance, do you have them associated with your financial life?

_____

_____

5- Check, at the end of the initial 7 days, to have all the income and expenses made in your expense manager.

6- You must end the week having the 4 piggy banks designed, remember that this creative act will allow you to develop a new meaning to content (knowledge) that we have already read, but that we need to assimilate. Reread chapter "Managing abundance," page , of section

7- At the end of week 1 write in your log:

What do you feel? What sensations appear with the first movements?

_____

_____

What new things motivate you?

_____

_____

What concerns, questions and thoughts appear in your mind?

_____

_____

WHAT DOES MONEY MEAN IN MY LIFE?

Write what appears in your log. These expressions, even if they are contradictory or you may consider them simple and/or important, will be of considerable value as we move forward.

_____

_____

_____

_____

_____

_____

_____

_____

Week 2

1- We will start by reading the chapter "Lack and abundance" from part 1 on page .

2- Write down resonances of the theme, freely express what happens to you:

Thoughts	Feel/Sensations

3- Answer:

Abundance:

What comes to your mind when I name you abundance?

Today, what aspect of your life is abundant?

_____

_____

Think about what your abundant life would be like.

Imagine it, enjoy it, write down what comes to you.

_____

_____

Lack:

What do you understand by lack?

_____

_____

What aspects of your life do you consider in a state of lack?

_____

_____

4- **Expense manager:** Continue writing down expenses and income day by day, verify if you have loaded the criteria for each expense and income in the correct place. It is important to be as precise as possible with this load of information.

5- **Money's story line in your life:** reread the chapter "How you perceive money", page , and carry out the activity.

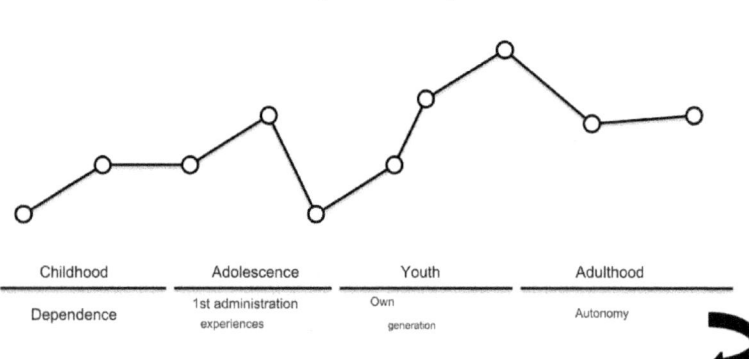

I suggest carrying out these tasks in a peaceful and quiet place, so you can concentrate and have a safe space to express yourself. Use music if it helps you concentrate.

What do you feel after doing the exercise about how money has traveled in your life history?

_____

_____

What milestones (experiences in your life) become most significant?

_____

_____

Can you perceive waves and moments of abundance on the timeline?

_____

_____

Can you perceive in your story places and scenes of lack that can be related to the significance of money?

_____

_____

6- **Emotional maturity with money:**

Ask yourself and answer yourself honestly:

Do you feel dependent on money?

_____

_____

Do you feel like you don't know how to generate and manage it? That you don't have much to offer?

_____

_____

Do you feel a lack of confidence in how to carry out what you do?

_____

_____

Do you feel autonomous in respect to money?

_____

_____

Reread in Part 1, in the Psychology of Money section, page, the segment referring to the importance of "life cycles."

Do you respond as a child, as a teenager, as a young person or as an adult, to the concept and management of money?

_____

_____

7- At the end of week 2 write in your log:

What do you feel, what sensations appear with this type of "movement" this week?

_____

What am I realizing?

_____

_____

How is your emotional world after these types of reviews?

_____

_____

Are you beginning to understand that the relationship with money is configured in our life history?

_____

_____

Week 3

1- We will start this week with a learning content "knowledge" of "the 4 keys of a rich person" do you remember that? Reread the section on Part 3, page .

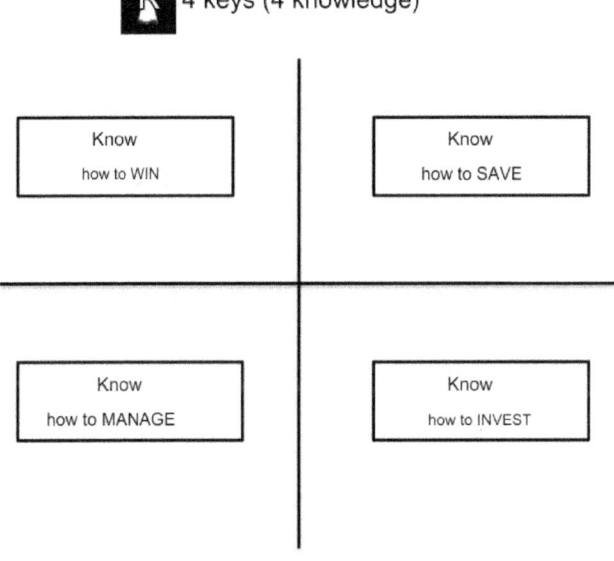

4 keys (4 knowledge)

What is my greatest strength? Which key do I need to add more quickly?

Concepts	Enter your priority
Gain	
Save	
Manage	
Invest	

Mark with a 1 the aspect that you most need to incorporate into your financial life; you can use 2, 3 and 4, always knowing that 1 is the highest priority and 4 is the lowest priority.

Our financial health will depend on this balance.

2- Beliefs:

Determine from your life story:

What enabling and limiting beliefs do you detect in your family regarding money?

_____

_____

What thoughts or phrases appear in your mind?

_____

_____

What strengths do you identify that you have in relation to money? In which aspect? What attitude? What knowledge?

_____

_____

Reread the section "the commands condition you" from Part 1, on page .

3- Tracking: Continue recording income and expenses day by day in a spreadsheet or expense manager.

Now pay attention to what usually happens with deferred expenses that we have from other months, which are often generated by installment purchases with credit cards. The goal of this exercise "is to know what expenses and income we have in this month of practice" therefore only write down on your spreadsheet what you spend this month (if you have installments, specify this month's installment in the expense manager).

4- Let's continue with beliefs

How do you feel when you detect the 3 most important limiting beliefs that you identify in your family?

_____

_____

From 0 to 10, 10 representing the most limiting response, how much do they prevent your progress?

_____

_____

Do you feel that your identified strengths allow you to obtain the keys of the rich man?

_____

_____

Can you realize the limiting mechanisms that always keep you in the same place?

5- Learning: resonances

<u>Write with authority:</u>

What do you want to learn?

How do you want to live?

What do you want your relationship with money to be like?

If you could build a new path for how money traveled in your life, what would it look like?

Are you willing to sketch out what the history of money in your life will be like from now on? Draw it with the enthusiasm of a child in your journal. Print new scenes of abundance on it (point out the milestones and experiences you dream of to achieve what you want).

6- Opening day:

A. Take some time to not think about anything and generate an experience of expansion, it could be, for example, visiting a park, going to a place alone for a weekend, looking for a space and opening up "an experience of abundance" it can or cannot be related to money.

Design it and write it down in your log.

Do it consciously looking for an opening goal.

Try to make yourself uncomfortable to open yourself to something new; reread the chapter "what is important is uncomfortable" from part 2 on page .

Write down in your log what you felt when trying to generate something with this type of slogan.

Was it easy?

_____

_____

Did you get stuck?

_____

_____

Was it impossible?

_____

_____

B. Detect a person in your environment who you consider has a good relationship with money:

Write down their name.

_____

_____

Describe their life.

_____

_____

What strengths do you detect on them?

_____

_____

What aspects make them abundant?

_____

_____

Is there a possibility of making an appointment with them?

_____

Dare to ask them for coffee to talk about topics related to the theme of money (remember that opening up with humility in front of others generates great opportunities and learning). Reread the chapter "Your only profit is your surplus" on the part 3 page.

7   At the end of week 3 write in your log:

What do you feel, what sensations appear with this week's steps?

_____

_____

What am I realizing?

_____

_____

How is your emotional world after these types of actions?

_____

_____

Are you beginning to understand that the relationship with money can be renewed or redesigned?

_____

_____

Week 4

1- At the end of this week, we should have all the income and expense information for this first month in our expense manager.

What do you feel when you see the flow of your money organized?

_____

_____

Was it significant to achieve this follow-up during the first month of practice? Had you already done it?

_____

_____

If you did it consistently, surely it won't be so uncomfortable to enter this data, right? Thus, when we really practice, new habits are incorporated.

2- Now that you see the flow of your money, what do you detect?

Is the money you generate enough for your fixed costs?

___

___

Do you have surpluses, are they reflected on your payroll?

___

___

Check your spreadsheet or manager to see if you are aware of all the expenses you entered. Many times, seeing it reflected in the spreadsheet, you can have conclusions like, did I spend so much money on fuel for my car this month? I had not realized this expense.

Point out the points that catch your attention the most.

___

___

3- Emotional:

Check if you consider that any of the expenses that are on your spreadsheet fulfill the function of "emotional compensation"; many times, we spend money to compensate for other types of voids (emotional).

Can you identify some of these offsetting expenses? Write them down.

_____

4- Thank yourself with a specific reward for the constant work you did in loading the flow of your money for 30 days in a row. "Our brain likes rewards, it's like it records that the actions performed are rewarded."

Write down in your log the prize you will give yourself.

_____

Do it this week.

What do you feel when you do it?

_____

_____

5- Reread the section "the two ways to win" in the page .

Do you have surpluses?

_____

_____

Do you feel like you manage your fixed costs well?

_____

_____

Can you make surpluses with better management?

_____

_____

What aspects would you like to correct for next month?

_____

_____

What decisions would you like to make so that your administration is more dynamic, balanced (emotionally)? Write down your decisions.

_____

_____

6- Interaction activity:

Detect someone in your environment who you consider is good with money, who is neat, stable in this sense.

Describe it in your log.

_____

What aspects do you point out as positive?

_____

_____

What limiting aspects do they have?

_____

_____

Ask them for a coffee/conversation to ask them how they manage themselves. Write down valuable resources that they can share with you.

It is important to have these meetings with others. They allow one to open the opportunity to learn for oneself and with the other, asking for feedback on what virtues those around us have, and realizing that the other is usually willing to help us.

7- **Piggy banks:**

Let's go back to the 4 piggy banks that you built in preparation for training, you remember right? Observe them like a trophy in front of you. We will now work with them; (Savings, Investment, Enjoyment and GIVING Piggy Banks).

Based on your entered data.

Have you made profits this month?

_____

_____

Remember that profit is always the surplus of money you obtain after deducting all fixed costs.

Is there profit?

_____

Write it down in your log.

_____

Do you like the number ($) you see?

_____

Do you understand that it is equivalent to the merit of the effort you made during these 30 days of generation with your work?

_____

What is happening to you emotionally? Write it down.

_____

Piggy banks and surplus:

Reread in part 3, the chapter "Managing abundance" of the page

A- Set aside 50% of your earnings for savings (remembering that savings are not touched).

B- Invest 20% in some asset, looking for a quick return of money (fixed term, surety, FCI.), some banking instrument already installed that is easy to operate. If you don't know about the topic, ask someone, it will be easy to incorporate it. The idea is to establish a small difference, but the focus is not on profitability at this moment, but on the exercise of taking money to invest and doing it concretely. This in practice breaks down many prejudices that we have related to the concept of investing.

C- Allocate 20% to enjoyment, plan some outing, buy yourself clothes, something that you feel you have deserved for a long time. Design it, write it in the log and conclude by writing down:

What do you feel when you invest in ENJOYING?

D- The remaining 10% seek to use it for GIVING, seek to design and put that money into something that really helps others, some cause, a donation, the purchase of something that makes life easier for another person, a gift; an action that allows you to practice this altruistic sense in yourself.

E- Design the activity, write it down, experience it and write how you feel when you manage to do it.

_____

_____

Month 2

Week 5

1- The first action to start month 2 is to take stock of month 1.

Write 10 important elements that stand out from all the comprehensive work of month 1.

Of those 10 points, choose 3 and write them down with color and capital letters in your log.

Describe in your log 3 valuable experiences that you have been encouraged to do in the first month of training. Maybe also some experience, that as a result of the movement made, came into your life.

2- KEY to WIN "Go ahead and generate."

Earning/generating money initially results in what you have to give (skills) and emotionally, in how you value yourself (how you sell yourself).

Determine in your log what your area of influence is. Reread the explanation <u>Influence zone</u> on the section page 4 keys of a rich man.

What is your passion?

_____

_____

What is your talent?

_____

_____

What is your value to your environment?

_____

_____

Dare to do this work, it is key that you know where your contribution and your strength are.

Determine your value proposition in a paragraph (record it in your log).

_____

_____

3- Value yourself:

Is it difficult for you to quote your services?

_____

Do you find it difficult to ask for raises when you deserve it?

_____

Do you make midterm financial plans to determine the profits you project?

_____

_____

4- Action:

Perform an exercise that will allow you to experience your assessment and your value proposition.

If you are an entrepreneur, you have certain ranges to quote your services and products, encourage yourself to quote 10% higher than the rest, seeking to experience more merit for your work.

_____

_____

Do it practically and see what happens.

_____

Most likely they will approve of the 10% increase.

_____

How do you feel when experience confirms your worthiness?

Can you understand that merit depends on your decisions?

Are you encouraged by your value proposition to generate a new pricing system that consolidates your merit?

If you work with a salary, be encouraged to ask for a benefit, an increase, recognition for the value you provide in the organization. Conduct an experience with criteria that allows you to make yourself uncomfortable to put into play the value you have to give.

Write down in your log what you feel when you do these experiences.

_____

_____

5- **Follow-up:** Continue recording your income and expenses in your expense manager. In this follow-up, remember the change goals that you wrote down in week 4 in your log.

6- **Gain:**

What do you need to learn to make more money?

_____

_____

Do you always move in the same social circles?

_____

_____

Do you renew your value competencies?

_____

_____

Are you into generating business plans?

_____

_____

Do you defend your value propositions?

_____

_____

7- At the end of week 5 write in your log:

What do you feel, what sensations appear with the self-assessment steps this week?

_____

_____

What am I realizing?

_____

_____

How is your emotional world after these types of actions?

_____

Are you beginning to understand that your relationship with money can be renewed or redesigned if you dare to value yourself more?

Week 6

1- Abundance map: Let's reissue the 4 pillars of abundance. Reread the section "Abundance and balance" of the page

2- Try to be honest in how you measure the percentages in the following table, being able to become aware of your balance in life currently:

Priority	Physical Life (Bodywork Health)	Mental Life (Mental and emotional health)	Spiritual Life (Transcendent Sense)	Financial Life
100%				
75%				
fifty%				
25%				

Mark with an X to manage the percentages.

3- Value stocks:

What do you want to improve in your physical life?

_____

_____

What do you want to improve in your emotional life?

___

What do you want to improve in your spiritual life?

___

What do you want to improve in your financial life?

___

Choose one of the variables and design an action to address improvements.

Write it down in your log, describe the improvement actions.

Do them.

Write down the results and track what you feel when you feed aspects of your abundance.

___

___

4- How would you like to balance these elements so that your life is abundant?

Describe that percentage.

_____

_____

What decisions do you need to make to achieve that balance?

_____

_____

What are you willing to give up, if necessary, for your life to achieve that balance?

_____

_____

5- Write down in your log:

Choose from your environment 4 people who represent each of the elements of abundance, bring them to your mind.

Describe in your log, what are each of them like?

Physical abundance (health):

_____

Emotional abundance (mind and emotion):

_____

Spiritual abundance (transcendence):

_____

Financial abundance:

_____

_____

5- Scanner:

Which of the people do you identify with the most?

_____

_____

Who do you feel most distant from?

_____

_____

What do you need to learn or do to start incorporating characteristics of the people you admire?

_____

_____

Write down these goals:

_____

_____

6- Create a high-value experience:

Without telling anyone, go out into life as the person you admire. Try, as if you were an actor, to build the character you are trying to incorporate.

For this exercise we made the first description, if you can take the character with which you feel the least identified, the experience will have a good impact.

This will allow you to do deep action work, as Jung says, "the integration of a shadow," everything we perceive belongs to us; some aspects are recognized "in light" and others in "shadow."

But why do they draw our attention?

_____

_____

Practice as if you were that person.

Visit the social and relational orbits that they visit.

It allows you to break down the idea that you are what you think you are.

If you do it, you will be surprised by the experiences that begin to emerge in your life.

7- Start writing down in your log what you think and feel when you dare to make this type of perceptual displacements.

8- Resonating:
How do you find this week's experience?

_____

Do you feel like you can build your future?

_____

When you decide to move forward, does your past weigh a lot? Do you feel lighter? More enthusiastic?

_____

To close this week, write in your log, what does **abundance** mean to you now?

_____

Dare to write an original paragraph, unique to you, that truly represents you.

_____
_____

Week 7

1- Read in part 1 the chapter "Finding the dinosaur doesn't change you" in the page .

2- Reflect in your log:

What stories from the past are you clinging to?

Can you see how that past justifies why you can't decide to change today?

3- **Perform a ritual:**

Write on a piece of paper the stories that you understand have limited you in relation to money (you already have this map).

Are you willing to leave them behind?

_____

_____

Could you live without them?

_____

_____

Bury the paper wherever you like, return to the earth what no longer has vitality in your life.

Notice what you feel when you perform this ritual.

4- **Designing future:**

Reread the chapter of part 2 "Educate your mind and your heart" in the page .

Can you see that change is possible?

_____

_____

Do you realize that it's just about taking action?

_____

_____

Do you realize that it is about moving towards the future with a desire to learn?

_____

_____

5- **Make the "treasure map" collage**

Take some cardboard, magazines, various items, glue, scissors, fibers, pencils, etc.

Creatively build what you want your abundant life to be like.

Design your future, the more detail you put, the more impact the exercise will have.

Perhaps you can accompany it with suggestive music that allows you to focus even more on the goal. Let's remember that the limbic part of our brain works with the senses. Every new sensation will be captured as part of the new.

Take all the time you need.

Write down how you feel after finishing the artwork of your future.

_____

Write down in your log what comes in your mind, in your feelings and in your body (sensations).

_____

_____

6- Reread to consolidate the exercise in the chapter "you write the future" in part 3 on page .

7- Remember to continue writing down the flow of money in your expense and income manager and above all, pay attention to the administration of your fixed costs, ensuring that there are no unnecessary leaks.

What appears in you with the concrete possibility of working for your future without so many excuses from the past?

_____

_____

Venturing into the real, into true possibility, can also generate fear. What do you perceive?

_____

_____

Week 8

1- Reread the <u>Chapter of the 4 ways of living</u> from part 3 on page .

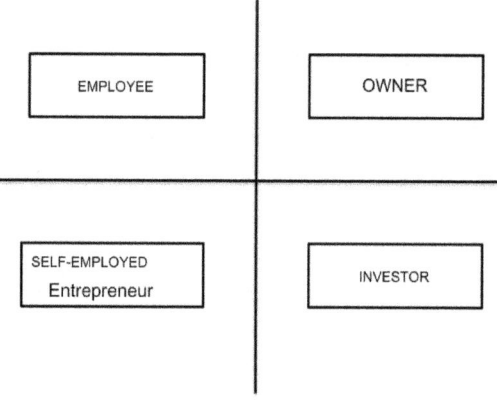

Can you notice where you are?

_____

Try not to let value judgments interfere:
Are you looking for excessive security?

_____

_____

Are you looking to be independent and original?

_____

_____

Are you looking to build teams to achieve great things?

_____

_____

Are you looking to be analytical and practical in how you get what you want?

_____

_____

2- **Change gaps:**

Determine, which quadrant do you want to start incorporating into your life? What way of living do you want to experience?

_____

_____

Each quadrant has a learning in itself, try to find what you need to incorporate at an attitudinal and content level.

3- Read the chapter "<u>Cross the surf</u>" of the page

Try to identify, what is your true purpose for crossing the surf?

_____

_____

What really awaits you on the other side?

_____

_____

Can you keep the treasure map collage you made in your mind?

_____

_____

4- Reread in part 2 the chapter "<u>Bridges to change</u>" page in part 2.

Discover:

What are your change enablers?

Can you add any more of those described in the chapter?

_____

_____

Is there an enabler you have, but aren't using?

_____

Choose 3 enablers (bridges to change) that you need to take to improve your relationship with money.

_____

_____

5- Experience:

Have an experience that challenges you, no matter how simple it may be, that takes you to a point where you need to stay to achieve its purpose.

Sometimes it can be a physical exercise that tests your ability.

Write down the experience:

_____

When you are at the resistant point, what thoughts come to your mind?

_____

If you stay, if you dare to be brave, you will surely find enablers that allow you to get through the surf.

_____

Which are they?

_____

_____

6- Administration:

How are your fixed cost management coming?

___

During this month have you been able to achieve the goals you set for yourself?
___

Do you have a profit at the end of this month, a surplus as a result of your good administration?
___

___

If you achieved it, identify and write down what you feel.
What do you realize?
___

What do you perceive at the end of two months of conscious order with the flow of your money?
___

___

7- Resonances:

How do you feel about what you have learned and experienced in this month of work?

_____

_____

Write, what elements do you take away from these 4 weeks?

_____

_____

Remember to redistribute your surpluses into the four piggy banks of abundance. If you are improving, encourage yourself now to set a profit goal for next month as a result of generating more money.
Write down the goal in your log.

_____

_____

Month 3

Week 9

1- Start by stating in your log:

What are you planning to do this month on top of everything you have been doing to generate more money, to consolidate a growing shift in your income?

Use your creativity to generate a little more $ with this goal.

The amount of money you generate is not initially relevant. The important thing is conscious movement.

Write it down.

2- Describe the actions you need to take to achieve this. Make a step by step agenda.

3- Reread within part 2, the chapter "Design your new habits", in the page .

    Review the 10 topics outlined in the chapter and adapt it to the experience you have chosen.

4- Meditation:

    Do quantum meditation. Those that calm the mind and place the desired image at the center of the meditation.

    Try to place there how you would feel about the challenge you set for yourself.

    Try to move towards that future and feel what sensations appear in you.

    Write down in your log what appears:

_____

_____

5- Expansion day:

   Dedicate a space to make contact with nature, an experience where thoughts of "doing" do not occur. Notice what you feel:

   Can you achieve it?

   _____

   _____

   Can you open yourself to your environment?

   _____

   _____

   Can you connect with another reality that is not just what you want?

   _____

   _____

   Can you feel part of something bigger?

   _____

   _____

   Answer each of the questions in your log.

6- To achieve the challenge you set for yourself, write down in your log what orbits or people you need to connect with, relate to.

"When you are locked inside yourself it will be very difficult to achieve something new."

7- Tell someone what you set out to achieve this month of work. This will make your internal commitment gain "social" strength and will help you break points of resistance.

Write down in your log who this person will be.

Week 10

1- How do you manage your time?

Reread in part 3, the chapter "If time is not enough, you are in lack" in the page .

What are your time eaters?

_____

_____

Who are your time givers?

_____

_____

2- It is important to know where our energy is going:

Can you identify on what you lose focus?

_____

_____

What are those activities, places or people that drain your energy?

_____

_____

Write them down in your log.

3- It is important to know where our energy is vitalized:

Can you identify which activities give you energy?

_____

_____

What interests capture your attention and productive concentration?

_____

_____

Write them down and highlight them with color.

4- Decisions:

Are you willing to "let go" of your time eater and focus on what is important?

_____

_____

What things are important to you?

_____

_____

Write them down, defend them, elaborate them.

5- Make a time use map in your log, where you identify the activities, places and people that give "vitamin" to your life. Always make reference to these points in your agenda.

Draw it in your log.

6- Always remember that "<u>Interest is the measure of action</u>." Reread in part 2, this chapter on page .

7- Ending the week, write down and highlight your week:

What relationship do you find to time and abundance?

_____

_____

If you save time, how do you use it?

_____

_____

Should I have time left over, with a surplus?

_____

_____

Does it have a relationship with money?

_____

_____

Write down in your log what comes to you.

Week 11

1- Investment key

Have you ever invested money?

_____

What comes to your mind when I talk to you about investing?

_____

Do you see it far away? Nearby? Possible?

_____

_____

2- If we return to the 4 elements of abundance in which you invest in yourself:

Write down below: Highlight where you invest time, energy and money.

Physical abundance (health):

_____

Emotional abundance (mind and emotion):

_____

Spiritual abundance (giving with transcendence):

_____

Financial abundance:

_____

3- Review, study and add technical elements that facilitate financial language. Reread the chapter of "Financial education" on page , part 3.

Try to go deeper and begin to complement it with tutorials, training, books, that facilitate financial language, which as we well know is very much in line with the emotional management of our life.

4- Indicate in the log the concepts or elements that you would like to learn regarding the technical content of finance. Go deeper.

5- Make an investment experience in your financial life:

> Extract $ from the investment piggy bank to be able to carry out a financial investment experience:
>
> A - Investigate what instruments are available on the market.
>
> B - Investigate Brokers and banking instruments that allow you to buy shares, negotiable obligations, bonds, and different operations that allow you to obtain differences by "placing" money.
>
> C - Take the necessary risk to set out to learn something that may be very new.
>
> D - To understand investments, create a broader map, the possibility of generating strategies by combining and diversifying your investment portfolio into different "baskets."
>
> Write down in your log how you feel doing this experience.

_____

_____

6- What is it like to invest energy in yourself?

Reread the section "<u>Know how to invest</u>," from the chapter "The 4 keys of a rich man" in part 3, on page .

How much do you value yourself now?

_____

Do you understand the most comprehensive meaning of investment?

_____

_____

Can you connect it to feeling worthy of more slack for yourself?

WHAT DOES MONEY MEAN IN MY LIFE?

What would happen if your income tripled as a result of good investments?

If you made the right moves, you will realize that it is not difficult to invest in yourself. It's just a matter of you deciding.

7- If you had to have a coffee with money,

What would that meeting be like?

What would you ask it?

Reread the page , the section "Have a coffee with the money."

Week 12

Last week of this three month sprint of concrete actions.

1- Remember that "<u>Nobody is a prophet in their own land</u>." Reread the chapter in part 4 on page .

It is important to understand that the learning path is not written.

Do you dare to write it outside your comfort zone?

_____

_____

Do you dare to introduce yourself to new scenarios where you are new for yourself and for others?

_____

_____

Do you dare to have the humble gesture of wanting to ask everything, to be able to go deeper?

_____

_____

2- By now your income and expense tracking should be a new habit in your life. Is it?

_____

_____

The administration of your 4 piggy banks of abundance begins to gain dynamism and correct use.

Can you see how abundance is organized?

_____

_____

3- You begin to understand that much of what is new is achieved by "DOING," venturing into the new.

Do you feel that's true?

___

___

4- Experience:

Choose a person in your environment who you perceive is in need of this type of learning.

Analyze their psychological profile. Handle yourself with empathy.

Organize some points that you have learned and summarize them in a table, order them.

Make an appointment with that person and try to provide what you didn't know 3 months ago and see what happens in you and in the person when you try to generously provide them with what you now know.

Write it down in your log.

___

___

5- Never forget that "<u>your talent is valued in the right context</u>" page . Choose well where you want to be located to be valued.

Describe the new orbits where you will move from now on.

_____

At least stand out 10 new spaces.

_____

6- Read the chapter "<u>balance is what defines your freedom</u>" from part 4 on page .

What decisions are about to make to achieve the balance you need?

_____

Write them down, even if they don't appear strongly yet.

What does freedom mean to you?

_____

_____

7- From this month, highlight 3 points that reached you the most. Write them down.

Finishing the training:

Can you detect specific learnings regarding money?

_____

_____

Do you feel that you have improved your connection with money?

_____

_____

Can you now understand its true function and purpose? Reread the chapter "Have a coffee with the money" of the page

_____

_____

Write who you would like to pass this book to, to continue this wheel of good, in terms of the integral meaning of what money means.

_____

_____

Final activity

Write, what does money mean to you now?

After reviewing, taking action, learning and practicing, did your meaning of money change at all?

Write it down:

Warnings

$

Opportunities are lost out of fear

Fear is an ally when it functions as an enabler, but when its force governs our lives, it often paralyzes us.

The warning lies in understanding that there will always be fear in any change, it is part of learning.

It is important to be aware of how fear can enable opportunities or inhibit them. We will leave as an annex the "chapter on courage and fear" (Book *Abrite Camino*) to delve deeper into the topic.

Practice what you understand

The truth is that if the resources presented in this book are not put into practice, we will not achieve true and complete learning.

As we explained in the chapter of "the three brains," if we only focus on understanding knowledge (neocortex) and savoring that sensation (light bulb) of realizing something important, and we do not put said content into practical experience, the learning will not happen, and neither will it happen that that knowledge becomes a habit for us. Therefore, if we do not "do" what we learn, nothing new will happen.

Be prepared to practice, at first you will surely be a little rustic and some mistakes will be necessary to take the first steps; but it is key to understand that our learning system needs concrete practice to incorporate what knowledge understands. **Remember, if you feel stuck it is because you are not practicing.** By setting ourselves in motion with knowledge we begin to experience the desire to align our thinking, feeling and doing in the same channel; and when this happens, paths open and we access high-value opportunities.

Find and release

Referring to the chapter "finding the dinosaur doesn't change you," on page , it is important to know how to delve deeper into the causes; the warning would be "deepen what is fair and necessary," since if you fall in love with causes from the past, you remain fixed on them. Go deeper to understand and then move towards the new, towards the possible learning, towards the construction of your future, where the good decisions of this present will lie; **decide now what you want and build it; the past dissolves with the force of your conscious decision.**

Value each step

As we already know, gratitude is the great virtue that allows us to achieve the balance that gives us freedom. The importance of valuing each step in your development and financial education will be vital to understand that consistency in any area of your life is achieved step by step. Shortcuts are allies of anxiety and haste, which usually thwart the true desire to improve ourselves.

Value your time

Life passes in time.

Try to channel all these learnings always based on the balance of the four elements of abundance (physical, emotional, spiritual and financial), time managed with this sense will surely give you content to your life.

The warning here is "be careful when it comes to money." I have observed many life imbalances when we begin to be successful with money. As it is a force that we do not know and do not yet manage, sometimes we can spend unnecessary time in projects of greed, power and egotism. Be careful with this point, which is the cause of many deviations throughout history.

Nobody is a prophet in their own land

$

Think big

This phrase contains many aspects to delve into, but I want to highlight it because it will be important to keep in mind that we do not achieve many of our dreams in close environments. What usually happens is that people who don't know us that much, value more objectively aspects of what we can provide, and those close to us fail to take in the new shoots we have to share.

Although this may seem illogical, it is totally logical, and I would even say natural. It is because the people close to us often have us defined in a perceptual framework of what we give, the profession we have, the social scale we occupy, etc.; so when we tell them, as it was in my case, that if I were a good musician I also wanted to dedicate myself to business consulting, helping people to have a better quality of life, they looked at me strangely, and without saying it they thought: You are dedicating yourself to adding value to a company as a consultant? Why don't you continue with what you know how to do?

So, it is not because of a lack of affection or intention that perhaps at first, they do not see new possibilities of what we want to achieve as potable, but rather we are perceptually predesigned for the other, in how we have manifested ourselves in life so far.

Suggestion: Only very few of your closest environment will see your potential for the new thing that you want to conquer and change.

Objectively look for people who know what you want to incorporate, learn from them, train yourself, good advice from these people will give you confidence, since it will be more objective; and one, being not so emotionally involved, will not enter into psychological games of external validation.

If you want something new you will have to cross the fence, expose yourself, leave your comfort zone definitively. The opportunity for it to be in a different and new environment opens the possibilities for it to be achieved, since in a scenario where no one knows us, we can "act" new ways of how to proceed and bring to light various aspects that we have hidden waiting to be expressed. It is not in vain that at a costume party, anyone who does not know how to dance, behind a mask, becomes Michael Jackson.

Look at the different experiences in your life, where you were encouraged to be different, and you will find that it was far from your most everyday circles, where we somehow felt safer, but also more restricted. Break with those logical traps that condition us, and if you want to change something in your life, be very clear that no one is a prophet in their own land.

Later, when you have conquered other lands, they will recognize you as an illustrious citizen, but in the meantime, work in silence, build solid foundations of trust with yourself and with people who know how to objectively see your talents and your aspects to improve.

In business life it often happens that a regional manager is fired, with the criterion that he does not have the necessary skills to perform his role, and two weeks later the competition hires him in the same position. After a month, the same company that fired him wants to rehire him, doubling his salary, because now that they see him with perspective contributing value to the competition, they begin to value him. **This is a clear example of how when the prophet is effective in another land, the country claims him as the best, but weeks before banished him for lack of merit. That's how it works, life itself.**

So, prepare your rags, channel your prophecies and train yourself to walk towards other lands where you can test and experience the potential that lives within you. It will be a great adventure to realize that you can achieve everything you set out to do if you find the context, the will and the sense of improvement necessary to break the barriers with yourself.

Cross the surf

$

Your strength and the sea

I really like taking time to go to the sea, I usually go to an apartment that has a window almost on the beach, there I usually venture out to write and concentrate on creative processes. I usually play by telling myself that I am the Argentine Neruda, remembering the beautiful visit I made with my wife to Isla Negra, in Chile, a place where the writer had a beautiful house, now a museum, facing the Pacific Ocean. On the guided tour we did, we entered his room, where he also used to write, and his bed was 45 degrees facing the window that looked directly onto the furious and tireless ocean. Beautiful postcard among other additions that give a framework and scene to his development as a writer.

Returning to my maritime place, the rhythmic sound of the sea is like a mantra that induces the generation of valuable ideas. In this place I wrote several chapters of this book, I still remember how the images and ideas to share appeared.

Between ideas, I sometimes withdraw my attention from what I'm doing and stop to observe how surfers try to challenge themselves against the lively waves that roll out on windy days, prior to the storms that suddenly appear.

What I want to highlight from my observation is the effort that these athletes make in crossing the surf, before preparing to catch the waves. I observe in that crossing with the sea the times when their strength falters and they are defeated face again the force that attacks the titan of the waters.

Once they cross the surf, the sea seems to offer other possibilities, from the shore it seems to be contemplated serenely. There the athletes move more freely, and the forces of the waves already hint at respecting their merit by not unloading on them the torrent of their sharp breaking waves.

This whole image brings to mind the analogy of when we want to change something in our lives. Whenever we propose something new or difficult, there will be a wave in equal proportions that will oppose us to test our strength, our intelligence and our empathy, to overcome the challenge posed by our own desire to improve ourselves.

I really like the analogy with water because it is an area where uncertainty is more present than in other areas, and it gives an emotional framework to the experience that makes it more meaningful. We are soul beings and 70% of our body is made of that same element, water.

I also remember, now that I cite maritime images with such prominence, an Argentine expeditionary that I admire and that I have had the pleasure of knowing personally. I am referring to Alfredo Barragán, who crossed the Atlantic in 1984 with a raft of logs, joined by plant ropes, without a rudder and with a sail, accompanied by 4 crew members with the desire to verify that Africans hundreds of years ago had done the same course.

What I want to highlight is what they asked him in a journalistic article: had he defeated the sea? He, with the eloquence that distinguishes him, responded: *"It is impossible to defeat the sea, trying to defeat it is going to the shipwreck, I studied the sea, and it let me sail in its waters because it understood that we knew it, because it saw that we did nothing to violate it."*

That's right, sometimes crossing the surf does not require strength, but rather another type of knowledge that allows us to cross it, and this is what I want to show, that comprehensive work with ourselves, with money or with other valuable content, requires of specific knowledge, which are the first enablers to try to achieve something, but it is also very necessary and decisive to want to improve ourselves in each learning.

This last condition is not taught, it is felt, it palpitates, it is perceived in the pulse of life and at the right moment.

Your talent is valued in the right context

$

Value yourself

A few days ago, I came across a video on social media showing a violinist with great expertise making music on a subway train in New York. The pieces that the instrumentalist played were really from someone who understood, who had studied to achieve expertise; people stopped because he attracted attention.

In my case, knowing music, I was able to realize that he had structure, support and content when it came to making art, precisely while I was watching the video, his level and the context he was playing caught my attention.

What the image showed was that people came up to give him some bills and coins that they kindly left on the case of his violin, which was resting on the floor.

He was playing music for 60 minutes in a busy subway station. At the end of that time, he had raised $30 for his art.

The video continues and then reveals that this violinist is a consecrated instrumentalist, who that night would give a concert as a soloist in a renowned theater in said city, where the cheapest ticket had a value of 150 dollars.

The scene showed in a very concrete way that *"Talent is valued in the right context."*

The same instrumentalist in different contexts, playing the same music, has another hierarchy, or level of attention, another framework, so that talent is recognized, in this case in terms of money, in a very different way.

It is very necessary that you learn to place yourself in spaces of merit. Places where what you have to give is recognized and valued.

I invite you to think that on many occasions we are very afraid to "shine," it is one of the evils that the world suffers from. I'm talking about a depersonalized glow, outside of all ego and narcissism. To truly feel recognized, it takes courage. This type of courage is what is needed to evolve, to risk taking dizzying heights that are worth it.

"If you don't show yourself, no one will see you, not even yourself."

Start by recognizing your talents, where "I am good," where I generate contributions to others. We all have this strength, that sacred fire that always pulses to express itself.

Then encourage yourself to be authentic and express what you have, what is closest to your convictions and tastes; some will help you get started, but you will have to take the last step alone.

As Herman Hesse says, **"You can walk in pairs, you can walk in threes, but you must take the last step alone."**

These moments of appropriation allow the necessary confidence to later venture to locate themselves in environments of greater deserving, where the same potential is more valued.

This is the most natural and authentic way to "sell yourself," to price our energy in front of others.

If you manage to do what you like, you will do it with pleasure, and that will allow others to observe the enjoyment with which you live; that is the best of magnets so that your life is filled with opportunities.

I also advise you to make a list of the contexts where you would like your value to be recognized. Dare to put a $ value on what you have to give, double that value, see how you feel, double it again, do you think it's a lot, right? Maybe they won't accept you anymore. Don't be afraid, try putting different values on what you have to give, you will be surprised when they accept values that you didn't imagine, and that after doing your job well, they want to hire you again.

"Learn to eat on sidewalks and at banquets." There's nothing wrong with making music in a city subway. They are different experiences, where whoever stops to listen to you is sometimes worth more than any money they can pay you in a prestigious room.

Learn to understand that contexts are created by us for something, find the meaning of each context, look for the benefit and learning that it implies, and thus everything will be more conscious, and you will learn to value yourself in the appropriate context.

.

Balance is what defines your freedom

$

Freedom

Freedom is an internal state that since immemorial times it seems that humanity has longed to achieve; almost like an end, which is tinged with plenitude, enjoyment and expansion.

The truth is that if we were objectively measured, after 80 years of life, how many minutes of freedom have we experienced? The answer would be a little discouraging; therefore, it does me good to think that freedom is not a point of arrival, nor is it a permanent state. I perceive it as a warm breeze that usually appears when we walk at our conscious pace, on our own feet, trying to achieve our chosen healthy conquests, always venturing to learn.

Therefore, freedom appears for those who commit themselves to what they really want. More than conquering it, freedom is felt, palpable in the most sensitive textures of our perception.

Financial Freedom

It is a concept that has been heard more and more strongly in recent decades. I understand that the thriving new generations, with more criteria of autonomy and confidence, have collaborated in integrating financial life and quality of life into the same category, allowing for a broader framework of possibility to create an abundant life, that is, a life where physical, emotional, spiritual and financial health are a beacon to follow and nourish. In the past, productivity and money, in certain cultures, inhibited people from developing their most intimate concerns. Today we seem to perceive a more sensible integration between what we want and what we do; rather, what is wanted is the basis of what is later done. This consequently generates more complete, happy, empowered and abundant people.

This is why financial freedom begins to make more sense. Technically we achieve financial freedom when we have reached a certain consistency regarding money and good and growing administration of it; in simpler terms, when we no longer have to worry about busily generating money, but rather we have already acquired the necessary knowledge to spin the wheel where the money generates itself. Therefore, this possibility is totally achievable, and it is just a matter of starting to practice and gradually incorporating valuable resources, practicing them and generating habits of abundance.

Balance

Balance is the great sage of the film, since it is who defines the possibility of freedom.

How does this work?

Balance occurs when the expectations we set for ourselves are consistent with the knowledge we have to achieve them; that is to say, that the goals that we decide to face are possible to achieve, because we base them on skills and knowledge already assimilated, which allow us, through effort and action, to achieve them.

If my expectations exceed my field of action, a certain frustration and incongruence begins to exist between the effort made and the lack of achievement.

I have seen many people frustrated by placing their expectations too unclear. Having everything to be free, by setting more horizons than possible, they condemn their happiness to an excessive goal that they cannot achieve.

This is why balance defines freedom, since the sound judgment of how to accommodate your contribution is what generates the opportunity and possibility of abundance.

In financial terms, balance is decisive when learning, since "the marathon" involved in achieving financial freedom requires many portions of freedom that are achieved step by step, knowing at each step how to balance the expectations of each learning.

Comprehensive financial freedom does not depend on the amount of money you have; on several occasions, a lot of money generates very heavy slavery. The possibility of deciding is what allows us to find a life in accordance with who we long to be. We could say then that freedom is achieved when the elements of abundance are balanced in our lives.

Dare to free yourself, to build and decide your freedom.

Synthesis 4

4th Part: PRACTICE

- Method: review, act, learn, practice
- Value warnings
- Find your new place
- Courage: Cross the surf
- Your talent: Learn to value yourself
- The balance for freedom

At the end of the day, it is all about what we have accomplished and what we "should" accomplish. We have two ways of doing it, improvising (spontaneous) or effectively, although excessive improvisation is not a friend of consistency.

You can follow my suggestions for habits and methods to learn and develop actions, you can also create your own; but without them you cannot build.

Let's think about building a future as if it were a building, we cannot improvise the calculation of materials, everything would collapse like a sandcastle next to the waves of the sea.

It is not difficult, it just requires time, repeating actions until we incorporate them on autopilot, but it is also important to get good suggestions. If we lie to ourselves by saying that we like to sleep in the morning, it is because we have forgotten how romantic it can be to get up to see a sunrise with the person we love. Yes, I used the word "lie" because sometimes we lie to ourselves and force behavior. I know people who did not like the morning, but as they placed pleasant activities at that time, the person feels energized. Ask yourself how you have felt on trips to places you have wanted to visit.

This book is about the meaning of money, and ultimately it is a work that will help you manage abundance and ward off lack. Habits and methods are needed. It's that easy.

If I find an activity attractive and I start repeating it, over and over again, I incorporate it into my life. We must be generous with those around us. Saying that I can't learn something, or that it is difficult for me to develop a habit, or that this or that other thing is difficult for me, we are underestimating ourselves, but mainly we are not taking care of the people around us.

Life is based on energy principles, I don't want to bore you with this topic, but good energy attracts good energy. When we begin to grow, we energize those around us, and a virtuous circle is formed.

It's about GIVING.

In this part 4 we have extended our reading to a process of interaction, with questions, with exercises to solve. Proposing 12 weeks of questions and activities to be recorded in a log is an invitation to produce habits, and if it is combining the reading of sections of the book it is to sustain them over time. The time one uses to reread is a time to imprint concepts, it is our immersion activity, to assimilate concepts.

A synthesis tries to summarize a corollary, it is to reinforce a concept, let's try to manage money, a diet, or our relationship with others, at the end of the day it is about having good habits and methods to make them grow.

There is a practical issue that we cannot fail to illuminate, when we begin to breathe well, sleep relaxed, eat healthy, save, invest, manage, earn, we develop abundance and spiritual, physical, emotional and financial health; and that's when life begins to smile at us.

No matter the circumstances, they educate our resilience.

I know it is not easy, that is why there are people who can help us in all areas, let's seek support. Let's not be greedy, let's not try to do everything alone, if we need engineers and architects for a house, we can also have coaches, mentors and health professionals for our lives.

I will share something with you, help others and you will see that life itself begins to help you.

I remember a person who complained about money, he didn't do it explicitly, but he always had a hard time paying for things. When he began to help others earn a lot of money, that abundance began to flow into that person. He now lives in Italy, he once earned the equivalent of 20 salaries, when he made another person earn more than 100 salaries. Yes, it works more or less like this, we receive a % of what we produce in others, it is like a net margin. I'll let you think about it...

Integration

$

Live what you want

After going through several chapters and topics related to money, what do you feel when we are almost finishing this attempt to bring this content to you from various points of view?

How does it feel to connect money to your life? To the experiences that since we were children we had to go through with this indicator of value, which gave the opportunity to achieve some dreams, which prevented the achievement of others, and which in other experiences was not necessary to dream and take what we needed. In those moments when we were looking into life, there was a value indicator that put a price on our toys. Without a doubt, an element that was in the fabric of our history and will continue to be. This is why it is so important to relate in the best way with this ally ($), who will often accompany us, giving us the peace of mind necessary to face life's circumstances, which may be, the latter, more important than a simple handful of tickets.

Sometimes very necessary and sometimes inconsequential, this will be this faithful companion, who in this physical life we will not be able to avoid and evade from our daily lives.

Remember that the four elements of abundance generate our balance in life, and the wisdom with which you approach it will be an indicator of integrity for you and for everyone around you.

It will be essential that you can incorporate "the 4 keys of a rich person" to be aware of what you need to learn to have self-control in managing money.

It is important to highlight that I make analogies between money management and energy management, where time management is also shown as an indicator to be followed and measured.

Learning to manage abundance with our 4 piggy banks will give us the peace of mind that we are collaborating with aspects of security and scope for expansion in our lives. It will allow us to manage our days with planning in an orderly manner.

Mastering the value of money will free us from an infinite number of worrying thoughts that torment the vast majority of human beings. Mastering this concept does not require being a millionaire, it depends exclusively on consciously managing the resources that we have been able to generate and develop. Understanding this point will be of great relevance since this perspective will be from where we can achieve balance and the so-called financial freedom.

Try to make a synthesis of the knowledge that you were able to incorporate in this book, what you were able to experience, and finally what you were able to change in your life and/or what you are preparing to change from now on.

Remember that the future is not written and every drop of ink that you write on the pages of your life depends on you.

Epilogue

After incorporating new knowledge and practicing it, try to verify how you feel internally when you seek to carry out conscious learning.

This book represents a first step and a compelling path to try to address issues such as money, from a comprehensive perspective, allowing you not only to assimilate new resources and knowledge, but also to carry out a strong review and redefine the concepts that allows us to redesign the future that each one wants to build.

Without identifying dysfunctional mechanisms, it is complex to rebuild the new horizon. It is important to understand, and you have verified that "finding the dinosaur does not change you," you could verify that having a good orientation for "doing" reorganizes your present in a way, that "the old" becomes obsolete, allowing it to give it a renewing oxygen to the attitude of the new.

The book is also an honest invitation for you to continue with this type of learning, since the opportunity for growth that is projected when you begin to articulate valuable knowledge and verify in concrete terms that there is the possibility of changing your habits and building your own clear map of what you need and want to find is fathomless.

You will soon be able to experience the internal benefit you feel when you generously bring your changes and learnings to other people who may be in need.

The circle of mutual aid and genuine interest in a "nostrity" will give us the conviction that collective learning allows us to renew the bases of what is studied, generating new codes and cultural patterns that give a beneficial current to our daily life and our desired aspirations.

In the unique intimacy that an author and his reader generate, I thank you for your respect for having approached this work, which I created with dedication, so that it can reach those who may need and value it.

WHAT DOES MONEY MEAN IN MY LIFE?

Attachments

Courage and Fear

$

From the book
"Abrite Camino"
Santiago Netri & Germán Netri

These two energies, although presented in a very antagonistic way, have strong implications in the learning process.

At first glance we could classify fear as a negative energy and courage as positive energy; but this could only be appreciated in a superfluous way, since the two energies contain their "light and shadow."

Animal life. Fear-Dread

We could say that fear fulfills a functional mission in animal life. This energy has allowed all species to preserve their lives against the threat of their predators and possible natural disasters. In this sense, its instinctive function of preservation responds to the principles of nature and compliance with certain laws that seem to regulate it.

In the presence of fear, the following characteristics can be observed in animal life:

- Attention
- Observation
- Concealment
- Flight
- Defense preparation

All these characteristics are at the service of preserving the "real threat" to life that the animal suffers in this situation. We could say that fear recreates a kind of protection against possible dangers in the natural animal chain.

Courage-Aggression

We could not describe the concept of courage from the perspective of animal life, because this energetic force is unique to human beings.

Yes, it can be observed in animal life, in certain situations, for example, when a species confronts a prey in search of food, an approach that could be confused with courage, where the animal displays a **strong aggression**, decision to attack, cunning, speed, voracity, dominance and precise determination in the conquest of their goal, which in this case, would be to feed themselves, defend their territory and/or their offspring.

It is observed in nature that this aggression sustains life, allowing each living being to update itself, always with a tendency to grow and to provide perspectives of favorable adaptation for its species.

It is important to make these clarifications and distinctions between **Fear-Dread and Courage-Aggression,** since when analyzed from the perspective of the human being, these concepts deserve certain details.

Fear and courage belong to the power of the human being, since he is the only one capable of "thinking" for himself, giving this condition the possibility of generating a perceptual construction representing these two attributes.

Human fear

Fear is a force that can both preserve a person's life and also "paralyze" it.

From an "organismic" perspective, and in terms of preserving life, fear fulfills an instinctive function similar to that which recreates fear in animal life. This characteristic has also worked, almost autonomously, to try to preserve the human species. The human being flees when he feels that his life is at risk, he hides, he produces an adrenaline state where his attention is prepared when he feels threatened.

When the threat to life is "real" fear fulfills a perfect function.

The problem arises when the fear that human beings experience is on a chimerical level. When the threat you feel has subjective overtones, which are specific to psychology, they make the person flee from situations that often appear in life with clear growth goals.

Subjectivity of Fear:

As we have already seen in other chapters, human beings generate concepts from the experiences they live and experience. In psychological terms, we create constructs, introjecting concepts that we incorporate and fix in our perceptual system; where they have a strong emotional charge, from where we perceive and give meaning to each concept we recreate in our life.

These constructs begin to form part of *the identity* that we think we have.

Fear in its instinctive function of preservation also acts psychologically and will always try to "defend" what the person considers to be their identity (made up of said introjected concepts).

Now, if growth and evolution ask us "implicitly" in said progress, to review how certain experiences have been recorded and fixed, the "old identity" can feel threatened, and that is where, almost unconsciously, instinctive fear "makes us flee" and the possibility and opportunity to resymbolize its constructs is lost, which would allow you to update the perceptual field, new experiences that life presents to you to follow your growth and evolution.

So, we should always check before any experience, whether the fear is real or fictitious.

If the fear that is perceived is real, the individual is located in time-space and can analyze the phenomenological variables and find in their understanding that there is a real danger, there "well-applied fear" preserves it and takes care of it in its process.

On the other hand, if fear preserves and cares for certain prejudices and beliefs (old identity) that no longer update the person, its function is negative and defensive, preventing the individual from resymbolizing what they need.

That is where we say that human beings can become paralyzed by fear.

Courage

As we mentioned previously, courage is a force that is unique to human beings. It is closely related to our convictions. We could say that they are the ones that inspire courage.

Sometimes, it is observed that this force can appear in situations of adversity. For example: facing a catastrophe; where life is at risk, an overwhelming force sometimes emerges, which even surprises the person themselves, allowing them to go through difficulties that seemed almost impossible.

Although here, courage is presented in the person's behavior, their actions are triggered in response to an emerging situation, almost as an "unconscious response" where the individual takes note of the danger and acts. These types of experiences make courage move by "need"; and although its response is effective, there is no determination here that generates it. This entire process is unconscious and/or subconscious, leaving aside the person's own understanding and decision.

The value that we want to recreate and analyze has another basis of approach.

We suggest that courage has to be consciously activated, where one's own will is aligned with this force in search of the goal.

We say that the determination to "invoke" courage initially arises from the clarity of the goal and the strong convictions one has to follow the path towards those desires. This type of value is not always based on emerging needs, but rather on the strength of self-improvement that one has. This "value" fights against one's own limitations, giving another consistency, confidence and strength to the person and the purpose that inspires them.

Time

$

From the book
"Abrite Camino"
Santiago Netri & Germán Netri

What do we understand by time? Let's describe the concept a little.

From the Latin *tempus*, the word **time** is used to name a **magnitude** of a physical nature that is used to measure how long something lasts, which is susceptible to change. When a thing passes from one state to another, and said change is noticed by an observer, that period can be quantified and measured as time.

"Physical dimension that represents the succession of states through which matter passes."

"A specific period during which an action is carried out or an event takes place."

We could say that people's lives and the history of humanity pass in time.

It is like a conveyor belt where lived experiences are fixed, giving it an order, a sequence and a projection.

Although currently, in our culture, time is taken as a point of time organization that balances the different activities of the community; anciently wise civilizations perceived it in greater depth, giving it a sacred order in their worldview, where the concept not only allowed a certain order in their civilization, but also on an intra-individual level, revealing secrets contained in "time" that favored all types of evolution in an integral way.

Analyzing it from nature, every natural process has its time of gestation, maturation and death. In this process, time passes that allows it to be carried out.

Before the unit of time appeared, which obviously allowed man to measure, investigate and have influence over certain processes, there were the cycles of nature, where natural time could be appreciated (day and night, life and death) evidencing the first great step to understand that recurring cycles in life existed in nature. This observation then allowed us to generate a "time unit" and thus measure these processes and interact with them.

Time also has a subjective aspect that we cannot fail to name, where in any ordinary situation we can perceive this reality. For example: in a movie that conventionally lasts two hours, perhaps subjectively for one person, they may perceive that one hour has passed, and for another person three have; this gives this concept a highly subjective connotation of how time is experienced and experienced.

The union of times is another interesting approach to propose.

The idea of a **past-present-future** integrated time. If we manage to amalgamate these criteria we can reach the following conclusion:

Our pasts were at some point our presents. So, the present we are living in, perhaps is the past of our future, and that future a new present.

If we can understand that this moment, this present, is a consequence of our past, and we use all the experience collected, adding the current elements, to face necessary existential questions; not only would we be facing situations in the present, but we would also be doing so in the past and in the future.

If our present changes, our past is resymbolized and we promote a new future.

We insist that the concept of time contains more secrets and mysteries that have always worried humanity.

In reference to its administration and use, we are going to work with two approaches in relation to this concept:

Linear time and integral time.

Linear time is that unit of measurement that allows us to carry out short, medium and long-term processes, taking into account a single goal.

Being aware of this linear time, you can plan movements and strategies to achieve what you propose. Being aware of what happens in linear time organizes us, giving order and achievement to the different instances. The awareness of this time allows us to then review the actions carried out, extracting the necessary steps to elaborate, repeat and/or teach the achieved goal.

It is essential to manage this type of time very well since it allows us to generate clear progress indicators in the creation and deployment of what we seek to achieve.

Comprehensive time invites us to carry out a more comprehensive review of how more than one goal is achieved at the same time, without losing sight of any of the processes.

A perspective view, with optimal distance, that infers another angle to our strategic map.

Finding objectivity in the volume of activities is totally necessary to manage abundance.

Managing these two types of time (linear and integral) is a good starting scheme to channel sustainable growth; since linear time will ensure that the actions we take are well organized; and comprehensive time will give you a strategic and tactical map of what we need to achieve.

Santiago Netri

Director of ENTRAMA CONSULTANCY.

Organizational Consultant. Specialist in Change Management and Systemic Diagnosis. Expert facilitator in work team development. His experience as a consultant leads him to place special emphasis on effective communication, teamwork and leadership.

The arrival of a new paradigm with more humane and committed organizations demands new approaches in the treatment of your human capital. Entrama, our consultancy firm based in Buenos Aires, is made up of an interdisciplinary team of professionals who are experts in enhancing the human networks of all types of organizations.

- **Consultant** Internationally certified by BBA. in Organizational Counseling. Expert in Rogerian approach oriented to the corporate field.
- **Founder and director** of Entrama Consultancy http://entramaconsultora.com.ar/
  IG entrama.consultoria
- Ágora Global Consultancy Redarchy consultant member.
  https://agoraglobal.net.ar/
- **Co-founder of Abrite Camino** (Training for entrepreneurs).
  http://www.abritecamino.com.ar/

- **International Certifications**
    - International certification in Change Management. (Change Americas).
    - International Organizational Development Certification. (Change Americas).
    - BBA. international certification in Organizational Counseling.
    - Certification in Gestalt approach and personal development.

- International Certification in Systemic Coaching (Integrate HR – Talent Manager).
- Certification in crisis management and communication in work teams. (Tomeu Barcelo, Portugal).

- **Postgraduate teacher and trainer** of personal development (Holos).

- **Postgraduate teacher and trainer** in organizational consulting.

www.ingramcontent.com/pod-product-compliance
Lightning Source LLC
Chambersburg PA
CBHW050155230526
45470CB00001B/102